AACRAO 2016

Academic Record *and* Transcript Guide

NAME	HOME SCHOOL INFORMATION	GRADE POINTS	MAJOR
LOCATION	NAME AND ADDRESS	TERM GRADE POINTS	MINOR
IDENTIFYING CODE	SCHOOL CODE	CUMULATIVE GRADE POINTS	HONORS AND DISTINCTIONS
IDENTIFICATION NUMBER	DATE OF GRADUATION	NARRATIVE EVALUATION	PROFESSIONAL CERTIFICATION REQUIREMENTS
SOCIAL SECURITY NUMBER	NATIONAL TEST SCORES	DEMONSTRATED COMPETENCIES	
TAX IDENTIFICATION NUMBER	STATE-MANDATED TEST SCORES	ACCEPTED TRANSFER CREDITS	SATISFACTORY COMPLETION OF INSTITUTIONAL QUALIFYING EXAMINATIONS
MAILING ADDRESS	COLLEGE CREDITS EARNED IN HIGH SCHOOL	COURSES, GRADES, CREDIT PER COURSE	
HOME ADDRESS	PREVIOUS COLLEGES ATTENDED	CREDIT SUMMARY	ADVANCEMENT AND/OR ADMISSION TO CANDIDACY
DATE OF BIRTH	CONCURRENT HS AND COLLEGE ATTENDANCE	NONTRADITIONAL WORK	TITLE OF THESIS OR DISSERTATION
PLACE OF BIRTH	TERMS OF ATTENDANCE	GOOD STANDING	TRANSCRIPT ISSUANCE INFORMATION
GENDER	DATES OF ATTENDANCE	ACADEMIC PROBATION	
RACE AND ETHNICITY	COMPLETE WITHDRAWAL DATE	ACADEMIC SUSPENSION	COURSES IN PROGRESS
MARITAL STATUS	COURSE IDENTIFICATION	DISCIPLINARY SUSPENSION	DATE OF ISSUE
FAITH PREFERENCE	CREDITS PER COURSE	INELIGIBILITY TO RE-ENROLL	AGENCY OF INTERNSHIP AND EXTERNSHIPS
ENROLLMENT STATUS	UNIT OF CREDIT	CLASS RANK	
	GRADE		

AMERICAN ASSOCIATION *of* COLLEGIATE
REGISTRARS *and* ADMISSIONS OFFICERS

AACRAO 2016
Academic Record *and* Transcript Guide

American Association of Collegiate
Registrars and Admissions Officers
One Dupont Circle, NW, Suite 520
Washington, DC 20036–1135

Tel: (202) 293–9161 | Fax: (202) 872–8857 | www.aacrao.org

For a complete listing of AACRAO publications, visit www.aacrao.org/publications.

The American Association of Collegiate Registrars and Admissions Officers, founded
in 1910, is a nonprofit, voluntary, professional association of more than 11,000 higher
education administrators who represent more than 2,600 institutions and agencies
in the United States and in forty countries around the world. The mission of the
Association is to provide leadership in policy initiation, interpretation, and implementation in the global educational community. This is accomplished through the
identification and promotion of standards and best practices in enrollment management, information technology, instructional management, and student services.

LIBRARY OF CONGRESS
CATALOGING-IN-PUBLICATION DATA

Names: American Association of Collegiate Registrars and Admissions Officers.

Title: AACRAO 2016 academic record and transcript guide / American Association
of Collegiate Registrars and Admissions Officers.

Other titles: American Association of Collegiate Registrars and Admissions Officers
2011 academic record and transcript guide | Academic record and transcript
guide

Description: Washington, DC : American Association of Collegiate Registrars and
Admissions Officers, [2015] | Includes bibliographical references and index.

Identifiers: LCCN 2015040417 | ISBN 9781578581115

Subjects: LCSH: Universities and colleges—United States—Records and correspon-
dence. | College registrars—United States. | Universities and colleges—United
States—Admission.

Classification: LCC LB2341 .A145 2015 | DDC 378.1/01—dc23

LC record available at http://lccn.loc.gov/2015040417

Prepared by:

The Committee on *The AACRAO 2016 Academic Record and Transcript Guide.*

Committee Members

Susan E. Hamilton (Chair)
Assistant Vice Chancellor for Academic & Student Affairs,
Rutgers University, Biomedical and Health Sciences

Julie Ferguson, MPA
Assistant Dean for Student Affairs/Registrar,
Rutgers University-New Jersey Medical School

Martha Henebry
Director of Operations, Membership and Publications, AACRAO

Nora McLaughlin
Registrar, Reed College

Jessica Montgomery
Associate Director of Membership and Publications, AACRAO

Rodney Parks
Registrar, Elon University

Tara Sprehe
Associate Dean, Enrollment and Student
Services, Clackamas Community College

Susan Van Voorhis
Associate Vice Provost of Academic Support Resources
and University Registrar, University of Minnesota

Daniel R. Weber
University Registrar, Northeastern Illinois University

Contents

CHAPTER FIVE

TARA SPREHE & DANIEL R. WEBER

Transcript Services and Legal Considerations 39

CHAPTER SIX

SUSAN VAN VOORHIS

Security of Student Records 53

CHAPTER SEVEN

SUSAN VAN VOORHIS

Fraudulent Transcripts 63

APPENDICES

Foreword

The American Association of Collegiate Registrars and Admissions Officers (AACRAO) has long been concerned with the integrity, ease of interpretation, and technological and privacy aspects of transmission of transcripts.

The *AACRAO Academic Record and Transcript Guide* is only one of numerous resources developed by AACRAO to assist its members. The list of references, following the Glossary, highlights the pertinent ones.

The Association was founded in 1910. At the second Annual Meeting, held in Boston in 1911, a committee was appointed to "give further consideration to the problem of devising a uniform blank for the transfer of a student's record."

While initial efforts were focused upon the development of a uniform transcript blank for most colleges and universities, the aim since 1942 has been to agree on essential items of information which should be included.

Those essential items were listed in the 1945 *Guide* and in the 1947 reprint. The 1949 *Supplement*, reissued in 1950, added brief explanations or definitions for each item. The 1952 revision included discussions of transcript evaluation, forged transcripts, transcripts for teacher licensing needs, and a bibliography.

Additional changes in the 1959 *Guide* included advances in transcript design made in cooperation with the National Association of State Directors of Teacher Education and Certification. Significant contributions to this *Guide* were abstracted from a report entitled "The Recording and Reporting of Student Disciplinary Records"—a report that was developed jointly with and adopted by AACRAO, the American College Personnel Association, the National Association of Women Deans and Counselors, and the National Association of Student Personnel Administrators. Recommendations of the Association of Graduate Deans were also considered as to the arrangement of essential items.

The 1965 *Guide* included a formal resolution of the State Directors of Teacher Education and Certification concerning the acceptance of a transcript as a document to facilitate teacher certification. This *Guide* also incorporated the recommendations of the Committee on Improvement of Student Personnel Records of the Council of Graduate Schools of the United States, and addressed the use of "reproducing equipment" for transcripts. This edition also included modifications of essential transcript items, with explanations, and contained as an appendix "A Guide to Good Practices in the Recording and Reporting of Student Disciplinary Records"—a guide which was replaced by the 1970 AACRAO statement entitled *Release of Information About Students: A Guide*.

Through the 70s and 80s the *Guides* reflected the changes brought about by the passage of the *Family Educational Rights and Privacy Act of 1974* (FERPA), as amended, and also contained information and recommendations on continuing education and nontraditional education records. They differentiated between the content of academic records, the content of academic transcripts, and the content of other institutional records. They also responded to an increased need for security awareness by including, as an appendix, a self-audit of record and transcript policies and practices. Another appendix provided sample transcript forms to aid colleges and universities planning for revision of basic records systems and transcript production.

The 1996 Guide built on the distinction between academic records and academic transcripts by listing all components according to their suitability to appear on the transcript, or only in the database. It began using a four-level scale to evaluate each component for suitability for transcript and/or database: Essential, Recommended, Optional, or Not Recommended. This edition identified "disciplinary action" as an item that should be maintained by the institution in its database, but which should *not* appear on the academic transcript. Reflecting a new interest in the electronic exchange of data, the 1996 *Guide* added such a chapter. Other new features in the 1996 edition included an expanded section on nontraditional courses, a sample transcript key, and a suggested reading list.

The 2003 *Guide* updated the discussion of database and transcript components in chapter 3; addressed the current impact of FERPA and the USA PATRIOT Act on the release of student educational records; updated the discussion of fraudulent transcripts, security of records, and Continuing Education Unit (CEU) Records; and explained two standards for electronic transcript exchange: EDI and XML.

The 2011 *Guide* developed the discussion on best practices for electronic data storage and security training for staff, and included the results of a 2009–10 Survey of the AACRAO membership on current transcript practices and opinions. Information and Recommendations about technologies such as the PDF, newer XML, Internet, email, document imaging, and student information systems were woven throughout the chapters.

Certain practices were the center of extensive discussions (and slight modifications) by the *Academic Record and Transcript Guide* committee:

* Notation of SSNs, academic and disciplinary actions, and course mode of delivery on the transcript;
* Requirements for change of name and gender;
* Issuing duplicate and replacement diplomas; and
* Student option for issuing transcripts that show only a specific degree and supporting coursework when a student has attended both undergraduate and graduate or professional divisions within the same institution.

The Academic Record and Transcript Guide Task Force who edited the current *Guide* continued the discussion of these evolving issues and included, for the first time, a discussion of the extended transcript concept. This is a suggestion by professionals in the student affairs arena to expand the role of the transcript beyond the record of a student's academic performance in higher education to include co- and extra-curricular activities in which a student may have participated.

An Introduction to the Academic Record and Transcript

Julie Ferguson
Assistant Dean for Student Affairs/Registrar,
Rutgers University-New Jersey Medical School

Susan E. Hamilton
Assistant Vice Chancellor for Academic & Student Affairs
Rutgers University, Biomedical and Health Sciences

Historical Perspective

The office and functions of the registrar date back to the great medieval universities of Bologna, Paris, and Oxford (Quann 1979, 2). As early as the twelfth century, the beadle was an official who proclaimed announcements, exacted fines, and helped the academic operation run smoothly.

The first academic officer with the title of "registrar" was appointed in 1446 at Oxford University (Quann 1979, 5). That officer's duties were "to give form and permanence to the university's public acts, to draft its letters, to make copies of its documents, and to register the names of its graduates and their "examinatory sermons."

In the United States, at the first institution of higher education (Harvard College, established in 1636), the registrar's academic recordkeeping function was initially a part-time duty assigned to a faculty member. The position rapidly became professionalized, however, as student enrollment in colleges grew. Along with the college president, the treasurer, and the librarian, the registrar was among the first administrative officers to become a specialist (Quann 1979, 6). Among institutions belonging to the Association of American Universities, fewer than 10 percent had registrars as of 1880, but 25 percent had designated them by 1890, as had 42 percent by 1900, and 76 percent by 1910—the founding year of the American Association of Collegiate Registrars (AACR), now the American Association of Collegiate Registrars and Admissions Officers (AACRAO) (6–7). (AACRAO added "and Admissions Officers" in 1949.)

The modern-day Office of the Registrar exists to serve the needs of students, to respond to requests of the faculty and administration for data, and to safeguard the integrity of the institution's records and degrees.

Evolution of the Transcript Out of the Academic Record

In the nineteenth century, a college or university "student information system" consisted of two ledger books. One was a compilation of class rosters, with final examination and course grades posted by each name. The other was the "matriculants' book," with demographic information about each student, often: the home county, the parents' names, and the student's religious denomination.

Since all students followed the same curriculum, transcripts were not needed, and few were prepared. The registrar simply noted the degree received or, if the student did not graduate, the number of years of study completed. Such certifications were usually prepared as letters, in response to a request for information.

Around the turn of the twentieth century, spurred by the new elective system of course offerings and by the introduction of major and minor fields of study, colleges and universities began to shift the focus from the graduating cohort to the individual student. Records now consisted of a separate page for each student—a page which combined demographic information with a compilation of the student's individualized set of courses. All the pertinent information about any one student was contained on one ledger page. In the early years of the twentieth century, the ledger page became a record card. This document became known as the "permanent record card." The permanent record card was the major database of its day—a repository of much miscellaneous information related to the student.

The transcript is that extract of the student's record which reflects his or her academic performance at the institution. After World War II, with the increase in student enrollment, registrars often photocopied the permanent record card to serve as a transcript. Even in an era when privacy requirements were not yet codified in federal and state law, this was not an optimum system.

The Academic Record and Transcript Today

Today, registrars remain tasked with preserving the integrity of an institution's academic records. The use of student information systems, Internet, email, and document imaging have made it easier to produce and promptly disseminate information from a student's academic record and the student's transcript upon receipt of an authorized request. Nevertheless, registrars and records professionals are challenged to reconcile two competing demands: the need to provide accurate information promptly to various constituencies and the need to safeguard privacy.

In the *AACRAO 2016 Academic Record and Transcript Guide*, we have tried to educate the reader of the differences between "database," and "academic record or transcript," and make some distinctions based on the historical evolution of those concepts. Additionally, current issues that pertain to the maintenance and representation of academic records are explored. Fifty-four database and transcript components are presented, along with recommendations as to whether their use is Essential, Recommended, Optional, or Not Recommended in the database and/or on the transcript.

We hope that this work will be of immediate and continuing use to registrars and information professionals in a variety of settings and at all stages of their careers. Ultimately, it is the responsibility of the issuing institution to be certain that their records and academic transcripts are appropriate, contain at the least the essential data elements specified in this publication, and are consistent with the local, state and federal legal guidelines under which the institution operates.

Chapter Summaries

In order to facilitate easy use of this *Guide*, we here present a brief overview of each chapter.

Chapter One addresses current issues which continue to be worthy of discussion based upon practical concerns and/or changes in our culture, including the notation of disciplinary actions on the transcript and recording name and gender changes. Each issue is reviewed as a sub-section of the chapter.

In Chapter Two, we provide a list of data elements that will be helpful to records and registration officers in maintaining the distinction between information that is appropriate to be maintained in the database and the smaller subset of information that is appropriate to be placed on an official transcript. Note that in Appendix C, we present a "Self-Audit" exercise concerning what should, and should not be, included on transcripts.

In Chapter Three, we present a concise guide to the transcript key. We list 20 items that are essential to be included in the key, and seven optional items.

Note that we also present and explain the highlights of a survey that AACRAO conducted in the winter of 2014–15, concerning current institutional practice (Appendix A) and registrars' opinions as to what they considered to be best practice for an institution of their type (Appendix B).

Chapter Four is an expanded and updated discussion of the transcription of nontraditional work. It draws a distinction between identifying the origin of the coursework (recommended) and identifying the mode of delivery (not recommended). It discusses the transcription of various types of nontraditional learning including experiential and co-curricular learning, credit by examination, distance learning, study abroad, military education, corporate education, external degree programs, competency-based education, and continuing education. It also includes examples of how these can be transcribed onto the transcript.

Chapter Five updates the discussion of transcript services. It includes a discussion on best practices surrounding transcript requests, security features for transcripts, how FERPA, the USA PATRIOT Act, and the Solomon Amendment impact the release of student education records, as well as a discussion on electronic data exchange.

Chapter Six discusses the physical and electronic security of records, security training for staff, and additional safeguards and challenges in maintaining the integrity of student records.

Chapter Seven is devoted to identifying and preventing transcript fraud. In this chapter you will find a succinct summary of best practices to use when safeguarding the authenticity of a transcript or identifying a fraudulent document.

We also include eight appendices, including the results of the survey on transcript practices and best practice opinions, AACRAO's best practices for PDF transcript exchange, the results of the student identity preferences survey, a Self-Audit checklist, the Extended Transcript Framework, and sample electronic notifications for transcript exchange.

Finally, we also include an expanded and updated Glossary, an updated and annotated list of references, and an index.

1

CHAPTER ONE

Current Issues

Julie Ferguson

Assistant Dean for Student Affairs/Registrar,
Rutgers University-New Jersey Medical School

Susan E. Hamilton

Assistant Vice Chancellor for Academic & Student Affairs,
Rutgers University, Biomedical and Health Sciences

Current Issues

This chapter will address many issues that are currently under discussion at the institutional and national level. These topics have engendered much debate amongst enrollment, legal, and student affairs professionals, and include:

* Recording actions on transcripts,
* Use of Social Security Numbers in the student database and on the academic transcript,
* Recording name changes,
* Recording gender changes,
* Reissuance of diplomas, and
* Alternative credentials.

Results of the 2015 AACRAO survey of current practices among member institutions and opinions of individual registrars vary widely (*see* Appendix A, "Survey Results: Official Transcript Practices," on page 71 and Appendix B, "Survey Results: Opinion on Best Transcript Practices," on page 77). Readers of this *Guide* are encouraged to carefully review the results found in this survey to inform their policy decisions and institutional best practices. While various recommendations and conclusions are put forward, the decision as to how to best manage these matters primarily resides with each institution in accordance with their state laws.

Recording Actions on Transcripts: A Historical Perspective

Historically, U.S. institutions manually recorded student status information on permanent record cards. Once recorded, communicating this information on the transcript was unavoidable because the student's record and transcript were the same document.

In modern student records systems, however, maintaining documentation of an action that affects a student's status and recording it on the academic transcript are two separate and distinct activities. Beginning in the early 1970s, when electronic information systems made it much easier to generate a transcript as a separate document from the permanent record card, it was no longer necessary to record academic and disciplinary probation, suspension, dismissal, or ineligibility to re-enroll on the official transcript. In 1996 the recording of disciplinary actions on the transcript was identified as no longer a recommended best practice.

In recent years, some have called for a return to notating disciplinary actions and other non-academic information on transcripts, citing the need for an official transcript to reflect an unabridged account of a student's academic, disciplinary, and extra-curricular history at an institution.

Recording Academic Actions on Transcripts

As the transcript is a reflection of a student's academic performance at an institution, recording academic actions such as "good (academic) standing," "academic probation," "academic suspension," or "academic dismissal" on an official academic transcript is a long-held construct in higher education.

The decision of whether to include academic actions on a transcript should be based upon the historical practice and the culture of the institution. Factors to consider include:

✻ all of the necessary academic performance data, such as course grades, GPA, hours attempted, hours earned, semesters enrolled, etc., is detailed on the transcript, thus making notation unnecessary and, perhaps, redundant; or

✻ even with the presence of "keys" to the transcript, not all grading systems are immediately transparent, nor are the academic progress standards of the institution always clearly stated.

Opting to include or exclude academic actions on the transcript are both legitimate policies to hold. In the end, it is the recipient's responsibility to interpret and evaluate the information that is presented on the transcript in accordance with that institution's policies and practices.

Recording Non-Academic Actions on Transcripts

RECORDING ACADEMIC DISTINCTIONS, PERIODS OF NON-ENROLLMENT, AND NOTATIONS PERTAINING TO COMPLETION OF DEGREE REQUIREMENTS

The inclusion of academic distinctions (Dean's list, class rank, Latin honors), periods of non-enrollment, and/or interruptions in a student's educational activity (leaves of absence, withdrawals), and/or notations pertaining to completion of degree

requirements in a graduate or professional program (satisfactory completion of institutional or national qualifying examinations, title of thesis or dissertation, etc.) on the official academic transcript remains under debate amongst records professionals. It is often institutional culture and the student's program of study that determine whether or not these actions are represented on the official academic transcript.

DISCIPLINARY ANNOTATIONS

Disciplinary actions differ from academic actions in that they are typically defined as violations of an institution's code of conduct. They may include, but are not limited to, academic infractions (plagiarism, cheating, etc.) or misbehavior (harassment, sexual misconduct, substance abuse, etc.). Current debate involves the inclusion or exclusion of such actions on the transcript as a method of sharing behavioral information or protecting a student's privacy rights.

Survey data of current recordkeeping *practices* solidly demonstrates that the vast majority of institutions do not record disciplinary violations on the academic transcript. Ninety-five percent of survey respondents indicated that their institution's academic transcript does not reflect students' probationary status for behavioral reasons or students' ineligibility to re-enroll due to *minor* disciplinary violations and 85 percent indicated that their institution's academic transcript does not reflect students' ineligibility to re-enroll due to *major* disciplinary violations.

In disciplinary matters, detailed supporting information is not included on or with the transcript, thus making the notation non-specific and potentially punitive. In addition, the information does not provide the recipient of the official transcript sufficient information to distinguish the nature or severity of the disciplinary action. Therefore, students may be misjudged by the notations.

The *opinion* of records professionals regarding the inclusion of disciplinary actions on an academic transcript, however, seems to be shifting. When asked to provide their opinions about best practices even if their opinions differed from their institution's practices, 86 percent of AACRAO survey respondents indicated that the academic transcript should not reflect a student's ineligibility to re-enroll due to *minor* disciplinary violations, a difference of 9 percent from the institutional practice. Only 60 percent indicated that the academic transcript should not reflect a student's ineligibility to re-enroll due to *major* disciplinary violations, a significant difference from institutional practice of 25 percent.

Public opinion about the disclosure of disciplinary action in an academic setting has also changed in favor of more transparency. Recent criminal offenses that captured national attention have resulted in changes in state legislation. As of the printing of this *Guide*, two states, New York and Virginia, have passed legislation requiring that such notation be made. For those institutions that are mandated to notate disciplinary action on the transcript or who have chosen to do so, possible language used to notate disciplinary action on the transcript includes:

* May not register for non-academic reasons
* Student has been expelled effective mm/dd/ yyyy
* Student is on disciplinary suspension effective mm/dd/yyyy until mm/dd/yyyy
* Dismissed for cause by Dean of Students
* Fall 2015—Suspended (or Dismissed) for Disciplinary Reasons
* Fall 2015—Suspended (or Dismissed) for Academic Code Violation
* Disciplinary Dismissal—May not re-enter without permission of Vice Chancellor for Student Affairs
* This transcript reflects only the academic record of the student; this student currently is not in good standing and further information should be requested from the Dean of Students' Office.

This will likely continue to be a highly-debated topic and institutions are advised to consult their local state laws regarding requirements to record such disciplinary actions on the transcript. It is also advised that attention be paid to possible federal action in this area.

For institutions that receive transcripts without disciplinary notations and are concerned with whether or not an applicant has been involved with a disciplinary procedure at another institution, screening of students in the application process can be helpful. School officials can also request the student's disciplinary records from the sending institution. FERPA requires institutions to treat disciplinary records as part of the education record, and since the entire education record can be shared and reviewed by appropriate school officials, there is nothing preventing the sending institution from transmitting the details of the disciplinary records to the receiving institution. However, institutions still need to inform students of such disclosures, either in their annual notice of FERPA rights or by directly contacting the student.

PARTICIPATION IN CO-CURRICULAR OR EXTRA-CURRICULAR ACTIVITIES

Current discussions among higher education professionals have begun to include consideration of co- and extra-curricular activities on the academic transcript. Language around the issue refers to an "extended transcript" or "digital portfolio" to record such activities as "badges" or "micro-credentials" that a student might earn within or separate from a traditional course; including participation in clubs, teams, service-learning opportunities, and the like. Additional items for inclusion could be competitions, notations to indicate creative awards won, or projects completed beyond the traditional classroom.

Some of the push for such transcripts comes from employers seeking to know more about graduates than their academics would reveal. These extra activities would supplement or even augment courses and grades to enhance a graduate's employability and likeliness to be hired.

Detractors of this effort report that expanding the data included on the academic transcript to include such activities dilutes the purpose of the record and may even make it a *less* valuable tool for recipients. Additionally, such non-academic entries that might appear to be "enrollment" could enable students to access institutional resources or services (health insurance, health services, technology) without the requisite fee and tuition payments usually assessed, especially if the extra-curricular activities are the *only* activity for a particular term. Participation alone does not relay information about skills learned, outcomes achieved, or concrete learning that occurred. They caution against the transcript becoming a resume, as opposed to an account of demonstrated performance.

The creation and maintenance of a separate non-academic transcript is one possible solution for institutions to explore until more data and evidence can be gathered on this issue. Some student information systems currently allow for the capturing of such information, enabling institutions to provide a compilation report to assist students with this record-keeping across their enrollment history. As of the date of printing, AACRAO is researching emerging practices in identifying, collecting, and documenting student learning in the extended transcript (*see* Appendix H, "A Framework for Extending the Transcript," on page 103). More information and guidance on this topic is expected to be released in the near future.

SUMMARY

The decision as to whether or not to record the status of academic or non-academic actions, such as academic distinctions, periods of non-enrollment, completion of degree requirements on transcripts, disciplinary annotations, or participation in co-curricular and/or extra-curricular activities on official academic transcripts is a complex issue that warrants thorough discussion between the academic affairs, student affairs, and legal affairs offices at the institutional level.

Use of Social Security Numbers in the Student Database and on the Academic Transcript

For a number of years, the use of the Social Security Number (SSN) has not been recommended as a means of identifying students. Institutions are appropriately concerned with privacy issues and with the potential for identity theft.

In the AACRAO survey of current practices among member institutions, results show that:

❋ 82 percent of respondents use the entire SSN in their student academic database; and

❋ 95 percent have migrated to another student ID number as their primary student identification.

On the transcript, the survey found that:

❋ Only 13 percent of institutions use the entire SSN on the official academic transcript;

❋ 39 percent represent a truncated SSN on the official transcript; and

❋ 80 percent represent another student ID on the transcript.

SUMMARY

It is recommended that institutions collect SSNs as a secondary student identifier in the database. Regulations implementing Section 6050S of the Internal Revenue Code require that institutions attempt to collect and report SSNs and Individual Taxpayer Identification Number (ITINs) for use on IRS Form 1098-T for all students on whose behalf tuition is paid. In addition, this use of the SSN provides a convenient check on the student's identity, especially for common or recurring names. It also facilitates interface with external entities such as government agencies, other institutions, and testing companies.

The use of a complete or truncated SSNs on academic transcripts, however, is not recommended. The academic transcript is a confidential document, the release of which must be approved by the student. While the use of the entire SSN on the transcript might expedite the appropriate sharing of information, its inclusion may facilitate fraudulent misappropriation or theft of the student's identity.

Name Change Recommendations

There are several factors to consider when reviewing institutional policy on name changes: the status of the student (currently enrolled or former student), the desire to accommodate student wishes, the need to safeguard the integrity of the transcript, state laws on the issue, and the configuration of the student information system.

AACRAO surveyed members about common practice concerning documentation required for making official changes in name for current students (*see* Appendix G, "Survey Results: Tracking Student Identity Preferences," on page 99). The survey revealed that, of the 839 respondents to the survey, 74 percent considered presentation of legal proof, such as a marriage license or court order, minimally sufficient documentation to support making the change in name in the student's record. Fifty-nine percent found presentation of one government-issued identification document, such as a driver's license, passport, or social security card, minimally sufficient documentation to support making the change in name, whereas 18 percent found presentation of at least two government-issued identification documents minimally sufficient documentation to support making the change in name. Only five percent made name changes without requiring any documented proof of name change. Aside from making minor changes in name that are of an administrative

nature, AACRAO recommends requiring legal documentation of name change prior to making official updates in your student information system.

APPLICATIONS IN PRACTICE

Current Students

✳ *Recommendation:* All students currently enrolled at the institution should be granted the opportunity to change their names on institutional records upon the production of legal evidence indicating the name change.

✳ What type of documentation can be considered legal?

◆ Certified copy of a marriage license, court order, or dissolution decree reflecting the new name in full.

◆ At least one government-issued official proof of identity. In some states, a driver's license is considered an official proof of identity because one is not issued unless valid identification documents are presented. For foreign nationals, documents should be certified by the U.S. Embassy abroad or by the appropriate foreign embassy in the U.S.

◆ A combination of the aforementioned documentation.

Former Students

✳ *Academic Transcript and Diploma Recommendation:* Names should not be changed on the transcript or on the diploma, except when there has been a court-ordered change of name. Upon presentation of a certified copy of the court order, diplomas in the new name may be issued to the graduate.

✳ *Database Recommendation:* The new name should be added and used upon receipt of proper documentation as defined by the institution. This is especially useful for integrated data systems (for example, when alumni development wishes to address graduates by their most current name).

✻ *Pre-Database Recommendation:* Archived records residing in an alternate format *(e.g.,* microfilm, imaged, etc.) are difficult to change. Some states prohibit, without lawful authority, tampering with or altering of existing records, including expunging critical information. Institutions are encouraged to cross-reference such records to the best of their ability so as to provide continuing service to students in such a situation.

Re-Applicants

The new name should be applied to the current record including transcripts and cross-referenced with the former name(s).

Minor Variations in Names

The registrar has the discretion to accept minor changes in names *(e.g.,* spelling corrections or revisions) without requiring equal scrutiny of legal documentation. In such instances, the student may be expected to provide documentation such as a current driver's license with photo, social security card, or resident alien card.

GENDER CHANGE

A certified copy of a court order or documentation from a health professional that a gender change is underway is required if an official change in gender and name is to be permanently recorded on a student's record. Furthermore, consultation with legal counsel may be necessary concerning the requirements of state law. Regardless of the legal name and gender maintained in the student database, many institutions allow a student in transition to elect use of a "chosen name" or "preferred name" instead of their legal name on unofficial campus records and documents, such as course and grade rosters, online directory listings, identification cards, and other public institutional records and documents. Permitting use of a "chosen name" or "preferred name" reflects an institution's sensitivity to a student in transition.

In addition, institutions may wish to expand their databases to include gender codes such as "trans-man," "genderqueer," or "questioning" to accommodate growing numbers of individuals self-identifying as such. Some schools are also expanding the options for pronouns used to refer to students. Options in addition to "he" and "she" include "they," "zhe," and "ze" (*see* Appendix G: "Survey Results: Tracking Student Identity Preferences," on page 99).

Because of the significance of a change in name and gender, official records of former students should be changed as well, provided the certified copy of the court order or documentation from a health professional has been received and a cross-reference system is in place. No historical evidence of the gender change should be referenced on a student's official academic transcript. For new names on diplomas, see "Reissuance of Diploma Upon Change of Name or Change of Gender" below.

Reissuance of Diploma

REISSUANCE OF DIPLOMA UPON CHANGE OF NAME OR GENDER

A diploma may be reissued for a graduate whose name has legally changed. It is recommended that the new diploma have wording that the diploma has been reissued.

The reprinted diploma should carry the precise date the degree was originally awarded. For practical purposes, the signatures of the officials may be of those currently in office.

REPLACING A LOST OR DESTROYED DIPLOMA OR REQUESTING A DUPLICATE DIPLOMA

A similar procedure should be followed when a diploma is reprinted to replace an original that has been lost or destroyed. Students may request duplicate or second copies of their diplomas for framing in an office as well as at home, or to present to a family member. Such duplicates are recommended to be exact copies of the original diploma and do not need any indication that they are in any way different.

REPLACING A DIPLOMA AFTER AN INSTITUTIONAL NAME CHANGE

In such a case the suggested wording may be used:

Degree granted by Central State College on [date]. This institution officially became Central State University on [date].

Cross-Referencing

Records officers should have a well-designed cross-referencing system for student records. Such a protocol should accommodate official name changes for current students, for former students wherever possible, and indicate both former and new legal names while matching student identification or social security numbers to each name. This cross-referencing system is necessary to provide quality continuing service to students regardless of staff or policy changes.

Alternative Credentials

Some institutions have begun to issue certificates, similar to diplomas, which attest to students' achievement of particular areas of study. Monitoring these documents for accuracy and validity may soon become a challenge for receiving institutions, and a task for institutions named on them to verify.

Additionally, electronic diplomas printed by students for retrieval and presentation for employment and subsequent enrollment purposes have begun to emerge. These also present a risk for fraud and need monitoring by institutions.

Summary

It should be evident to readers of this *Guide* that current issues often remain "current" for many years as opinions, practices, and technology often impact records professionals' tasks for some time after their first emergence. It is advised that leaders of record offices keep in contact with professional organizations, listservs, advocacy groups, and other resources to gain truly current insights on any emerging issues.

Database and Academic Transcript Components

Nora McLaughlin

Registrar, Reed College

Database and Academic Transcript Components

The tables below include data elements that are key to student records. These data elements are listed as essential, recommended, optional, or not recommended for inclusion in the database and/or on the student's academic transcript. Because of the variability among student information systems, this is not a complete listing of all possible data elements, but represents those that are most common. The assessments are based on best practices, as reflected in AACRAO's Transcript Practices and Best Practice Opinions survey (*see* Appendix A, "Survey Results: Official Transcript Practices," on page 71 and Appendix B, "Survey Results: Opinion on Best Transcript Practices," on page 77). It is important to note that student databases include data that should not be included on a student's academic transcript, in order to protect student identity and to ensure that the record provides only information that is appropriate for the recipient.

Item	Data Element	Comments/Recommendations	Database	Transcript
INSTITUTIONAL IDENTIFICATION				
1	Name	▸ For multi-entity institutions, the transcript must reference the degree-granting entity. ▸ Any prior names of the institution should also be included in the transcript key for at least 10 years after the name change.	Essential	Essential
2	Location: City, State, ZIP Code, Telephone Number, Website	▸ Since some institutions use optical character recognition software to read hardcopy transcripts, it is recommended that these data elements are included on the back of the transcript so as to simplify the front content for ease of recognition.	Essential	Essential
3	Identifying Code	▸ It is helpful to the recipient of the transcript if one or more of the following identifying codes is noted on the transcript: ACT, CEEB, OPE ID or FICE code. When reported, the source of the code should be identified.	Recommended	Recommended
STUDENT IDENTIFICATION				
4	Name	▸ The transcript must contain the documented legal name of the student including first, last, and if applicable, middle initial. (*See* Chapter 1 for further information on recommended documentation for name changes.)	Essential	Essential

13

Item	Data Element	Comments/Recommendations	Database	Transcript
5	Identification Number	▶ Many states have legislation restricting the use of social security numbers as primary identifiers. It is best to issue alternate primary identification numbers as student IDs, given the use of social security numbers in identity theft.	Essential	Essential
6	Social Security Number (SSN) or Tax Identification Number (TIN)	▶ Compliance with the Internal Revenue Code requires institutions of higher education to attempt to collect the SSN for students for tax credit purposes. ▶ If collected, the SSN should only be accessible in the database by a restricted population of employees.	Recommended	Not Recommended
7	Mailing Address	▶ Unless the transcript is being issued to the student, a student's mailing address should not be included on the transcript. ▶ The mailing address data elements should include street, city, zip, state, county, and country, if applicable. ▶ Other addresses such as permanent, emergency, legal, etc. are optional, except as required by law.	Essential	Not Recommended
8	Email Address	▶ The email appearing in the database should be the institution's officially assigned email, if one is issued. ▶ Other email addresses may be stored and used to communicate with the student in accordance with the institution's communication policy.	Essential	Not Recommended
9	Date of Birth (DOB)	▶ The DOB is often used to match academic records at the receiving institution. ▶ The DOB in the database must include day, month, and year. ▶ Including the full DOB on the transcript may result in real or perceived age discrimination. It is recommended that only the birth month and day be included.	Essential	Recommended (month and day only)
10	Place of Birth	▶ While sometimes useful in establishing residency for fee purposes, it may be a source of perceived discrimination. ▶ It is essential to collect this information for international students applying for an F-1 student visa.	Optional	Not Recommended
11	Gender	▶ Institutions are asked to report this information for IPEDS. ▶ Some states do not allow for this data element to be a required field. ▶ In addition to female and male, institutions may wish to include other options such as transgender.	Recommended for institutional reporting purposes	Not Recommended
12	Race and Ethnicity	▶ Like gender, this data element is part of IPEDS reporting. ▶ Institutions may not mandate disclosure of this information from prospective or current students. ▶ Mandatory compliance of the use of the IPEDS race and ethnicity categories began in Fall 2010: (http://nces.ed.gov/ipeds/news_room/ana_Changes_to_10_25_2007_169.asp)	Recommended for institutional reporting purposes	Not Recommended
13	Marital Status	▶ Usually not relevant, unless the institution offers benefits to married students or their families.	Optional	Not Recommended
14	Religious Affiliation	▶ Information may be useful to campus activities, especially in church-related institutions.	Optional	Not Recommended
15	Disability	▶ Disability information should be maintained in the database, but only if reported by the student. Access to this information should be limited to a "need-to-know" basis.	Optional	Not Recommended
16	Citizenship and/or US Citizenship and Immigration Services (USCIS) Status for visa holders and students applying for federal financial aid	▶ The USCIS requires institutions to maintain and report up-to-date data through the SEVIS system on visa holders.	Essential	Not Recommended

Item	Data Element	Comments/Recommendations	Database	Transcript
DATA ELEMENTS USED AS A BASIS FOR ADMISSION				
17	Secondary School Graduation, GED, Home School Information, or Equivalent	▸ This data element should only be collected if needed as part of an admissions decision, financial aid eligibility, or for reporting purposes.	Optional	Not Recommended
A	*Name and Address*	▸ Data elements should include the name and full mailing address of the entity responsible for awarding high school equivalency.	Essential	Not Recommended
B	*School Code*	▸ CEEB or ACT code is necessary as a primary key for institutional differentiation in a database.	Essential	Not Recommended
C	*Date of Graduation*	▸ May be perceived as a basis for age discrimination. ▸ May be used in residency determination.	Essential	Not Recommended
18	Test Scores	▸ This data element should only be collected if needed as part of an admissions decision or for reporting purposes.	Optional	Not Recommended
A	*National Test Scores*	▸ Usually collected as part of the admissions process but not required for all admission decisions. ▸ SAT, ACT, GMAT, LSAT, MCAT, etc. score information may be proprietary information that cannot be released to third parties.	Essential if required by mandate or for admission decision, otherwise optional	Not Recommended
B	*State-Mandated*	▸ Collected as required in some states as part of the admission decision (example TAKS or STARR in Texas and OGT in Ohio).	Essential if required by mandate or for admission decision, otherwise optional	Not Recommended (unless required by state law)
RECORD OF WORK PURSUED AT CURRENT INSTITUTION				
19	Attendance			
A	*Terms of Attendance*	▸ Calendars should be described in detail in the transcript key or the course identification.	Essential	Essential
B	*Dates of Attendance*	▸ The database should include beginning-of- and end-of-term dates.	Essential	Optional
20	Complete Withdrawal Date	▸ Used to document a complete student withdrawal from the institution prior to the end of a term (after student has begun attending classes).	Essential	Recommended
21	Course Identification	▸ Includes department or discipline identifier, course number, course title, and special information, such as "honors course."	Essential	Essential
22	Credits Attempted per Course		Essential	Essential
23	Credits Earned per Course		Essential	Essential
24	Unit of Credit		Essential	Essential
25	Grades	▸ The grade earned in each course, whether used in computed averages or not, must be shown on the transcript. Exceptions must be included in the key.	Essential (including any changes that occur)	Essential
26	Term Grade Point Average (GPA)	▸ Grade Point Averages are computed by varying methods, especially with reference to repeated courses. ▸ May be dynamically computed.	Essential	Recommended

DATABASE AND ACADEMIC TRANSCRIPT COMPONENTS

15

Item	Data Element	Comments/Recommendations	Database	Transcript
27	Cumulative GPA	▸ If a GPA is computed and maintained by the school, whether cumulative or by session, and is reflected on the transcript, then it is recommended that the key contain information on how the average is computed (*e.g.*, how repeated courses are computed, whether courses are omitted from the calculation, etc.). ▸ Some institutions clearly state in policy that the transcript will reflect the cumulative GPA. ▸ It is sometimes required as part of cross-institutional articulation agreements.	Essential	Essential
28	Grade Points	▸ The product of grade earned multiplied by number of credits for a course.	Essential	Recommended
A	*Term Grade Points*	▸ Grade points earned each term.	Essential	Recommended
B	*Cumulative Grade Points*	▸ Grade points earned for all terms of enrollment.	Essential	Recommended
29	Narrative Evaluation	▸ Used by some institutions in lieu of or in addition to traditional letter grades.	Essential	Essential (if grades are not also recorded in letter or number form)
30	Demonstrated Competencies	▸ Non-classroom experiences for which credit is awarded. ▸ Note: Demonstrated competencies imply the awarding of credit; they should not be confused with demonstrated proficiencies (*see* Glossary).	Recommended	Recommended
RECORD OF WORK PURSUED AT PRIOR INSTITUTION(S)				
31	Accepted Transfer Credits	▸ This is an essential part of the database for degree audit and for academic advising. Coursework should be shown with dates when taken.	Essential	Essential
A	*Courses, Grades, Credit Per Course*	▸ Some institutions only transcript blocks of transfer credit hours and do not differentiate in the primary database the specific transfer course work details. ▸ Specification of transfer course work may reside in a secondary degree audit system.	Essential, but varies by transfer practice	Optional
B	*Credit Summary*	▸ Essential part of the database; may be computed dynamically. Credit hours accepted should be shown on the transcript, as should dates of attendance.	Essential	Recommended
32	College Credits Earned in High School	▸ Some states mandate that state institutions accept such credits.	Essential (if mandated)	Essential (if applied as transfer credit for the degree)
33	Previous Colleges or Universities Attended	▸ Institutions may choose to post this information only from institutions from which credit has been transferred. ▸ The history of the previous institutions attended may be helpful to the receiving institution, regardless of credit awarded.	Optional (unless required for admission or transfer credit)	Optional
A	*Name and Location of Institution*		Optional (unless required for admission or transfer credit)	Optional
B	*Period of Attendance*		Optional (unless required for admission or transfer credit)	Optional
C	*Degree Received*	▸ May be required for financial aid eligibility, admission, or transfer credit.	Optional	Optional

Item	Data Element	Comments/Recommendations	Database	Transcript
D	*Degree Conferral Year*		Optional (unless required for admission or transfer credit)	Optional
E	*School Code*		Optional (unless required for admission or transfer credit)	Optional
F	*Concurrent HS and College Attendance*		Optional (unless required for admission or transfer credit)	Optional

ACADEMIC STATUS

Item	Data Element	Comments/Recommendations	Database	Transcript
34	Good Standing	▸ Only academic statuses that interrupt a student's continued enrollment should be noted on the transcript.	Essential	Not Recommended
35	Academic Probation	▸ If academic standing is in use, this data element may be required for automated standing processing. ▸ Unless probation interrupts a student's continued enrollment, it should not appear on the transcript. Changes in academic status that interrupt a student's enrollment may include: Withdrawal, Suspension, or Dismissal. ▸ *See* Glossary. *See also* "Recording Academic Actions on Transcripts," in Chapter 1.	Essential	Optional
36	Academic Suspension or Ineligibility to Re-Enroll	▸ If academic standing is in use, this data element may be required for automated standing processing. ▸ For further discussion *see* "Recording Academic Actions on Transcripts," in Chapter 1.	Essential	Optional
37	Disciplinary Suspension or Ineligibility to Re-Enroll	▸ Essential on the transcript if mandated by state law ▸ For further discussion *see* "Disciplinary Annotations" in Chapter 1.	Essential	Optional
38	Academic Honors in Progress	▸ Institution-wide academic honors, not departmental honors or organizational memberships, awarded during a student's career may, at the institution's discretion, be recorded in the database or on the honors transcript. *See also* item 45, "Honors and Distinctions."	Optional	Optional
39	Class Rank	▸ Not always calculated and the means of calculation varies by institution.	Optional	Not Recommended

STATEMENT OF GRADUATION

Item	Data Element	Comments/Recommendations	Database	Transcript
40	Degree or Certificate Earned	▸ Title of the degree or certificate.	Essential	Essential
41	Date Conferred	▸ Date the degree is officially awarded. ▸ The month and year are essential; inclusion of the day is recommended. ▸ May be included only as "date completed".	Essential	Essential
42	Date Completed	▸ May be the same as date conferred. If not, this date should reflect the completion of degree requirements.	Essential	Optional
43	Major	▸ The CIP (Classification of Instructional Programs) code should be considered essential for the database but is optional for the transcript.	Essential	Essential (as the major), CIP code is optional

17

Item	Data Element	Comments/Recommendations	Database	Transcript
44	Minor, Concentration, Specialization, etc.	▶ Not all institutions offer minors and institutional policies vary as to whether the minor is included on the transcript. ▶ See Glossary under "Minor Area of Study."	Essential	Recommended based on policy
45	Honors and Distinctions	▶ These should be limited to academic graduation honors awarded by the institution and should not include membership in honorary organizations or other distinctions and awards unless expressly included in policy. See also item 38, "Academic Honors in Progress."	Essential	Recommended
46	Professional Certification Requirements	▶ Include only if part of degree requirements; specific test scores should not be reflected.	Recommended	Optional (unless required by state law or professional licensing)

SUPPLEMENTAL INFORMATION FOR GRADUATE AND PROFESSIONAL STUDENTS

Item	Data Element	Comments/Recommendations	Database	Transcript
47	Satisfactory Completion of Institutional Qualifying Examinations	▶ Essential on transcript if mandated by state.	Essential	Optional (unless mandated by state)
48	Advancement and/or Admission to Candidacy		Essential	Optional
49	Title of Thesis or Dissertation		Optional	Optional

MISCELLANEOUS

Item	Data Element	Comments/Recommendations	Database	Transcript
50	Transcript Issuance Information			
A	*Courses in Progress*	▶ List of courses in which the student is enrolled at the time of issuance of the transcript. ▶ May be very helpful to receiving entities. ▶ "In Progress" should be clearly noted. ▶ If courses in progress are not shown, the transcript may indicate whether the student is currently enrolled.	Essential	Optional
B	*Date of Issue*	▶ Necessary in order for the recipient to know whether the record is current. ▶ Sending information should be maintained for a period of time as an audit trail in compliance with FERPA requirements.	Essential	Essential
51	Agency of Internships and Externships	▶ May be useful for potential employers and for certification and licensure agencies.	Optional	Optional
52	Last Entry Notation	▶ The recipient can more readily determine whether the record has been altered.	Not Applicable	Essential
53	Extra-Curricular Activities	▶ Including involvement in student organizations, study abroad, etc. See also "Participation in co-curricular or extra-curricular activities," in Chapter 1.	Optional	Not Recommended (except as part of an enhanced transcript with a separate record for non-academic experiences)
54	Athletic Participation by Sport	▶ As required for NCAA or other similar organizations. See also "Participation in co-curricular or extra-curricular activities," in Chapter 1.	Essential for institutional reporting purposes	Not Recommended (except as part of an enhanced transcript with a separate record for non-academic experiences)

DATABASE AND ACADEMIC TRANSCRIPT COMPONENTS

18

3

CHAPTER THREE

Transcript Key

Nora McLaughlin
Registrar, Reed College

Transcript Key

A transcript key or legend should clarify the information presented on an academic transcript and provide guidance for understanding and evaluating that information. The key is a necessary and integral component of the transcript and is most commonly printed on the back side of the transcript paper stock. Electronic transcripts must include coding for effective transcript interpretation by the receiving institution.

If not included on the front of the transcript, it is essential that the following items be represented in the key:

* Name, address, and, if applicable, branch location of the institution
* Reference to institutional name changes dated within the past 10 years
* Relevant contact information, including telephone number(s), fax number, email address, website
* Institutional ID codes such as OPE ID, FICE, ACT, CEEB, etc. (if included, identify the code reported)
* Accreditation statement
* Calendar system
* Definition of enrollment terms (specify the approximate start and end date or length of term)

* Unit of credit (semester, quarter, other—if other, include the recommended means of translation to semester or quarter units)
* Grading system (*e.g.,* letter grades, numeric grades, Pass/Fail, etc.)
* Method of grade point average calculation (*e.g.,* A = 4, A- = 3.7, B+ = 3.3, etc.)
* Institutional policy on recording all courses attempted
* Institutional policy on withdrawals, transfer credits, incompletes, repeated courses, academic forgiveness and academic bankruptcy (if applicable)
* Course identification system indicating level (first-year, sophomore, graduate, etc.)
* Explanation of any unique or unusual academic policies or programs that are reflected on the transcript
* Effective dates and/or end dates should be included for each of the above items to reflect any changes to policies or information
* Method of certification as an official transcript (embedded security features in paper used, embossed seal, etc.)
* A warning against alteration or forgery

* Policy regarding eligibility to re-enroll (*e.g.,* academically eligible to re-enroll unless otherwise noted)
* FERPA rediscloure statement (see note below)
* Date of last revision to the key

The following are optional items that may be included in a key:

* Office to contact for student's disciplinary record (verify the institution's policy before including a statement)
* Definition of the codes or abbreviations used on the transcript
* Rules for academic probation, suspension, dismissal or other academic action
* Graduation requirements outline, *e.g.,* number of units for a degree
* Degrees awarded by the institution, and their abbreviations (if used)
* Requirements for institutional honors
* Information regarding consortium agreements, if applicable

FERPA Rediscloure Limitation

The AACRAO 2012 FERPA Guide suggests the following sample FERPA Rediscloure Notice for use on transcripts:

"In accordance with U.S.C. 438(6)(4)(8)(The Family Educational Rights and Privacy Act of 1974) you are hereby notified that this information is provided upon the condition that you, your agents, or employees will not permit any other party access to this record without consent of the student. Alteration of this transcript may be a criminal offense" (Rooker *et al.* 2012, 133).

CHAPTER FOUR

Nontraditional Work and Continuing Education Unit Records

Rodney Parks

Registrar, Elon University

Nontraditional Work and Continuing Education Unit Records

Nontraditional Work: An Overview

Both the practice of awarding credit for nontraditional educational experiences and the variation in their delivery suggest the need to define different types of credit clearly.

In this chapter, the most common types of nontraditional education are identified and described. In addition, examples are provided of how to record those types of nontraditional education on the transcript.

As institutions see a drop in first-time enrollment figures, some institutions have begun seeking avenues of providing nontraditional education to meet the needs of a changing student demographic. Nontraditional education includes programs that offer alternatives within or without the formal educational system and provide innovative and flexible instruction, curricula, grading systems, or degree requirements (Mayhew 2014). Developments in technology have vastly improved the delivery of these programmatic alternatives, making education more accessible to a broad array of learners. With pressure on institutions to increase degree completion, new approaches such as adaptive technologies, self-paced online courses, and other web-enabled courses are increasing. As a result, registrars often must take on more responsibilities to arbitrate, translate, influence, and record nontraditional academic work.

Examples of nontraditional education include experiential learning, credit by examination, correspondence study, distance learning, and external degree programs. Corporate education and continuing education can also be categorized as nontraditional education.

Utility of Policies Regarding the Acceptance of Credit

The evaluation of nontraditional learning experiences should be governed by clear and consistent policy. Colleges and universities should develop policies with careful attention to their interplay with the institutional mission, and then establish appropriate credit equivalencies where applicable.

A variety of resources are available to assist institutions with the evaluation of nontraditional learning, some of which are cited in this chapter. Because this publication is focused on academic records and transcription topics, it addresses evaluation only insofar as it affects the manner in which nontraditional learning and any associated credit equivalencies might be recorded on the transcript.

Calendar Considerations

Nontraditional education seldom conforms to the standard calendar of the institution. Learning may begin or end at any time, without regard to the institution's established semester or other term dates, complicating the process of reporting data, namely to the National Student Clearinghouse (NSC) and the National Student Loan Data System (NSLDS). While such reporting ought not dictate a college's practices, it is wise for all institutions to consider the impact for students when allowing such variations.

It is essential that institutions establish policies about how this type of learning will be recorded. If the learning experience is not offered in a standard calendar format, it is important that the starting and ending dates of the instruction or the prior learning experience be clearly indicated in the academic record.

Methods of Transcription

Nontraditional course credits are sometimes recorded via nontraditional methods, such as through the use of a narrative transcript and special grading symbols. Such entries are common for health professions, studio, and creative arts or practicum experiences, where a single letter or numerical grade is insufficient to indicate a student's learning or performance. Narratives are generally an evaluation of the student's overall academic achievement and the faculty's judgment, and can take up to six months to receive. Since nontraditional educational outcomes may vary substantially from those provided by traditional methods, it is incumbent upon the institution to record nontraditional education in a manner that allows recipients to make informed and reasonable evaluations of the educational experience.

Mode of Delivery; Identifying Origin of the Coursework

The issue of identification is anchored to two major factors: the mode of delivery of the educational experience and the origin of the work.

✱ *Mode of delivery:* The annotation of mode of delivery on the transcript is not recommended, unless credit is granted through a competency-based portfolio (*see* "Distance Learning" on page 30 and "Competency Based Education (CBE)" on page 34). However, some employers, governmental sponsors, or other interested parties may wish to know how a student received their course material. It is recommended that such information be provided as an addendum to the formal academic transcript.

✱ *Origin of the educational experience:* If the source of academic credit is not from the institution creating the record, the source of the credit should be identified on the transcript (*e.g.,* College Level Examination Program (CLEP) and Advanced Placement (AP)). Exceptions may apply where there are formal inter-institutional agreements. In the case of nontraditional learning at another institution, the practices of the recording institution should be set by institutional policy. The transcript may list all courses accepted for credit or may show only an aggregate amount of credit from a named institution for a specified period of time (*see* "Accepted Transfer Credits" on page 16).

Types of Nontraditional Education

There are many sources defining nontraditional education. Adapted from some of those documents are the following brief descriptions of various types of nontraditional education.

EXPERIENTIAL AND CO-CURRICULAR LEARNING

This category encompasses knowledge, skills, and values gained through life experiences, such as student employment, apprenticeships, internships, cooperative education, field experiences, leadership, and other creative and professional work experiences.

The source of credit for experiential learning should be noted clearly on the transcript so as not to be construed as credit earned in a traditional manner. Alternately, a separate co-curricular transcript (CCT) with its own legend may be produced as an addendum to the curricular transcript (*see* Figure 4.1, "Sample Co-Curricular Transcript," on page 28). This can be managed by Student Affairs, Student Activities, Community Service, or Career Services, depending on an institution's culture and resources. While a standard for the creation of co-curricular transcripts does not yet exist, most institutions have accepted the premise that experiential learning is a legitimate, valued element of their educational programs (Moore 2013). While some information stored on the co-curricular record appears on the academic transcript, most co-curricular records provide more details of the experience, such as the name of the employer and the number of hours completed during an internship. The institution's culture will be important when determining what experiences the institution certifies. Most often, students are responsible for managing their own CCT, similar to resume construction. A variety of mechanisms exist at institutions for handling this data entry, including paper or online forms for students to fill out. Many institutions permit students to change and update data they have already entered.

Validation of the data a student submits is problematic for institutions that want to certify the data to a potential employer. Similar to an academic transcript, verifications are needed so students do not misrepresent their experience. The importance of approval and information validation is critical if institutions hope to see these experiences benefit their students as they transition to the workplace. It is suggested that institutions be consistent in their descriptors to enable better interpretation by recipi-

ents of such transcripts. Students are often given the responsibility of obtaining the validation from the proper source. With a few exceptions (*e.g.*, copies of a certificate or some student organizations), the validations are given by faculty or staff members associated with the activity or members of the office that supports the transcript program.

Some institutions have taken the step to build co-curricular transcripts for the student by connecting the experiences to components of the curriculum. For example, when a research course is set up for an individual student, details about the experience may be added to the student's record to appear on the CCT automatically once the student successfully completes the course.

In recent years, some institutions have started combining the academic and co-curricular records to form a comprehensive credential that comprises more details on the college experience (*see* Appendix H, "A Framework for Extending the Transcript," on page 103). *See* "Participation in Co-Curricular or Extra-Curricular Activites" on page 5 for more discussion of the co-curricular transcript. It remains to be seen how these records will impact potential employers as institutions work to find new ways to certify attributes that employers are seeking.

CREDIT BY EXAMINATION

Included in this category are all credits earned through testing, namely college challenge exams, the College Level Examination Program (CLEP), Advanced Placement (AP) examinations; DANTES Subject Specialized Tests (DSSTs), the American College Testing (ACT) Proficiency Examination Program (PEP), Excelsior College's UExcel program, Straighterline, and the International Baccalaureate (IB) diploma program.

Credits awarded through such testing should appear on the academic transcript and include an indication of which test was used to grant the credit

FIGURE 4.1: Sample Co-Curricular Transcript

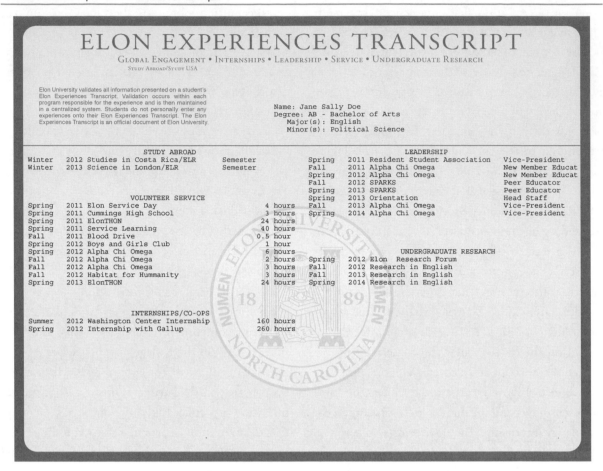

28

(*see* Figure 4.2, "Sample Transcript with Credit by Examination," on page 29).

PRIOR LEARNING ASSESSMENTS

While it is common for institutions to work with adult learners and assess credit from multiple institutions, these learners may also have gained college-level skills and competencies through work, military experience, volunteer service, or self-study. These students often express frustration at being asked to take college courses in subjects they may have already mastered. Prior learning assessment (PLA) is used to assess an individual's experiential and other institutional learning for the purpose of granting college credit, certification, or meeting prerequisites for higher level coursework (Klein-Collins 2014).

Institutions use a variety of different assessment strategies to evaluate prior learning for the purposes of awarding academic credit. Four generally accepted approaches include:

✳ Individualized Assessments where students prepare a portfolio of learning experiences and noncredit learning for faculty members with subject matter expertise to assess and determine the amount of credit to award.

✳ Faculty-developed challenge exams to allow students to earn credit for a specific course by taking a final comprehensive examination. Credit is generally only awarded for courses approved

FIGURE 4.2: Sample Transcript with Credit by Examination

Page **1** of **3**

Name: Sample Student
Student ID: 000001

University of Maryland University College
3501 University Boulevard
East Adelphi, MD 20783

UMUC Official Transcript

--- TEST CREDITS ---

Test Credits Applied Toward UG Bachelor's Degree		Test Date	Test Score
CLEP Subject Exams	Analysis & Interpretation Lit	09/01/1996	66.00
Dantes Exams	Public Speaking (SE821 025)	05/01/1997	69.00
CLEP General Exams	Humanities (Fine Art & Lit)	06/01/1997	640.00
CLEP Subject Exams	Intro Sociology	01/01/1998	59.00
Dantes Exams	Intro to Law Enforcement	10/01/2004	66.00
Dantes Exams	Intro Criminal Justice	10/01/2004	68.00
Dantes Exams	Drug & Alcohol Abuse	10/01/2005	64.00

		Attempted	Earned	Points
Test Trans GPA 0.000	Transfer Totals	27.000	27.000	0.000

through the college and university curriculum. (*See* "Course Challenge" on page 30)

✳ Standardized examinations such as Advanced Placement (AP), College Level Examination Program Exams (CLEP), Excelsior College Exams (UExcel), and DANTES Subject Standardized Tests.

✳ Evaluation of non-college programs such as ACE, NCCRS, and corporate programs that have been evaluated for college credit.

Awarding credit for learning outside of academe is a way institutions can accelerate degree completion for nontraditional learners. Data from the Integrated Postsecondary Education System (IPEDS) in 2012 indicates that 38 percent of regionally accredited 4-year and 41 percent of regionally accredited 2-year institutions offer "credit for life experience." The Council for Adult and Experiential Learning

(CAEL) has developed a national online portfolio assessment service that helps students develop a comprehensive learning portfolio and indicates a number of affiliated colleges and universities that accept credit for prior learning.[1]

Institutional practices on the posting of PLA credit vary. Some institutions show PLA credit on the academic transcript as transfer credit, while others post it as a course challenge (*see* "Course Challenge" on page 30). Still others post the course name for which the student earned credit through PLA with no additional markers noted on the transcript. Registrars are advised to post PLA as transfer credit with an informative identifier to indicate to any receiving institution that the entry contains PLA credit. (*See* Figure 4.3, "Sample Notation of Prior Learning Credit," on page 31.) It may be necessary to

....
[1] *See* <www.learningcounts.org>.

NONTRADITIONAL WORK AND CONTINUING EDUCATION UNIT RECORDS

29

place the PLA indication on the transcript if accreditors or licensure agencies require such information. School officials are encouraged to work closely with their associated organizations to ensure students and graduates are supported and compliant with discipline-specific requirements.

DISTANCE LEARNING

Distance learning courses are delivered through a variety of formats including entirely web-based, partly web-based, web-enhanced, interactive video, and podcasts. Distance learning courses should *not* be identified as such if they are applied to a degree program(s).

COURSE CHALLENGE

Many institutions have policies to allow students to earn academic credit for courses for which a suitable examination can be prepared and administered. Course challenge examinations are comprehensive tests of the material that is normally presented through a semester-long course. The examinations provide the opportunity to establish credit for competencies gained outside the classroom for which the academic credit has not already been earned. The grade the student earns on the challenge is entered and calculated into the average.

STUDY ABROAD

Study abroad consists of course experiences in another country either covered in a formal study abroad agreement or offered directly by the home institution.

These courses, or a summary of credit earned from these courses, should be identified on the transcript as a study abroad experience. Institutions affiliated with the host institution may post the equivalent grade earned on the academic transcript, rather than listing the courses as general transfer credit. At minimum, the transcription should include the country of study. If appropriate, the institution attended should be included as well (*i.e.,* the institution offering the courses in the host country.)

MASSIVE OPEN ONLINE COURSE (MOOC) CREDIT

A MOOC is a course of study made available over the Internet free of charge to the general public. There are currently over fifty MOOC platforms, each offering unique course designs and hosting services. Some platforms, like Coursera and edX, partner with accredited universities (Harvard and MIT among them) to deliver high quality content and learning support. In some cases, upon completion of the course, participants may pay an additional fee to receive a downloadable certificate that can be used for various reasons: traditional credit, resume updates, social media, etc.

Registrars are often faced with the challenge of determining transfer equivalency from a range of documentation provided by MOOC providers. Four commonly accepted methods by which students can pursue credit earned through a MOOC include:

✱ Completion of a MOOC that has been recommended for credit by the American Council for Education (ACE) or the National College Credit Recommendation Service (NCCRS).

✱ Completion of a MOOC from a regionally accredited college or university that awards credit for the MOOC.

✱ Institutional course challenge following the completion of a MOOC.

✱ College portfolio documenting a range of student learning activities (including MOOCs) that can be assessed by institutional faculty for college credit.

NON-CREDIT COURSES ON THE ACADEMIC TRANSCRIPT

It is not uncommon to see zero-credit hour courses listed on an academic transcript. Some institutions still use zero-credit courses as a means of placement testing to meet a prerequisite in a degree audit. Also, required remedial courses carry zero-credit

FIGURE 4.3: Sample Notation of Prior Learning Credit

Name: Sample Student
Student ID: 000001

University of Maryland University College
3501 University Boulevard
East Adelphi, MD 20783

UMUC Official Transcript

--- OTHER CREDITS ---

Other Credits Applied Toward UG Bachelor's Degree		Units Awarded
Portfolio Assessment Credit	EXCL 399 Property & Liability	3.000
Portfolio Assessment Credit	EXCL 399 Risk MGMT/BMGT	3.000
Portfolio Assessment Credit	EXCL 399 Lifelnsurance/BMGT	3.000
Portfolio Assessment Credit	EXCL 499 Human Resource Manage	3.000
Portfolio Assessment Credit	EXCL 499 Organizat. Behav/BMGT	1.000
Portfolio Assessment Credit	EXCL 499 Employment Law for B	4.000
Portfolio Assessment Credit	EXCL 499 Employee Training And	3.000
Portfolio Assessment Credit	EXCL 399 Employee Benefits An	3.000
Portfolio Assessment Credit	EXCL 499 Role of Human Resourc	2.000
Portfolio Assessment Credit	EXCL 199 PersonnelCounseling/	2.000
Portfolio Assessment Credit	EXCL 199 Tech of a Performance	2.000

--- BEGINNING OF UNDERGRADUATE RECORD ---

1997 Fall

Course	Description	Attempted	Earned	Grade	Points
EXCL 301	Lrng Analysis & Plng	3.000	3.000	S	0.000

		Attempted	Earned	Grade	Points
Term GPA 0.000	Term Totals	3.000	3.000	0.000	0.000

toward the degree but qualify students for financial aid. Such courses belong on the transcript. Some institutions will post zero-credit hour experiences if those experiences are a mandatory component of the curriculum. For example, leadership, service or global education may be a required experience within a curriculum where the student can satisfy the requirement without taking a credit-bearing course. Institutions rarely recognize these elements for academic credit unless granted through a competency-based portfolio of student experiences.

Institutions should work to be consistent as to which non-credit courses appear on the academic transcript and which do not.

MILITARY EDUCATION

ACE Military Guide

Many student veterans submit military transcripts that list service-related training and courses that have been reviewed by the American Council on Education (ACE). ACE convenes teams of teaching faculty who travel to military installations to evalu-

31

ate military training courses and occupation-based skills, knowledge, and abilities. Although colleges and universities are not bound by ACE evaluations and recommendations for the award of credit, this information serves as a valuable resource for those institutions that award credit based on military training and experiences. Learning that is eligible for review includes professional training, certifications and licenses, coursework earned at non-degree granting institutions, Advanced Placement exams, military training, experience, and coursework, and college-level examination program (CLEP) exams.[2]

Joint Services Transcript (JST)

Military experiences and education are presented on a synchronized transcript presenting data for the United States Army, Marine Corps, Navy, and Coast Guard. The transcript contains the following information:

✳ Personal service member data

✳ Military course completions—all courses that have been evaluated by ACE, with full descriptions and credit recommendations. *See* Figure 4.4a for a snapshot for military course completions on the JST.

✳ Military occupations—full descriptions, skill levels, and credit recommendations. *See* Figure 4.4b for a snapshot of military occupations on the JST.

✳ College-level test scores—CLEP, DSSTs, NCPACE, ACT/PEP, and Excelsior Test score data.

✳ Other learning experiences—additional completed courses and occupations not evaluated by ACE for college credit.

Not everything will appear on the JST, and it is recommended that registrars cross-reference the transcript with the ACE Military Guide. Additional information found in the ACE Military Guide includes course length, version, and related

competencies for select courses evaluated after 2006.

Department of Defense Forms

Additionally, the following Department of Defense forms may be presented by students while in military service or after discharge to assist with credit evaluation:

✳ DD Form 214 is the Certificate of Release or Discharge from Active Duty. It gives documentation of schools and occupations while in the service.

✳ DD Form 295 is an Application for the Evaluation of Learning Experiences during Military Service and is available to all active-duty service members.

✳ DD Form 2586 or VMET (Verification of Military Experience and Training) consists of ACE-recommended credit for military courses attended and occupational skills and training acquired while on active duty. It is designed as a transition tool to assist potential employers in the private sector. This form is best used with a DD 214.

✳ DA Form 1059 is a Service School Course Completion/Academic Evaluation Report that may be used to complement other records or when service courses are not recorded on official records such as the DD 214.

✳ Certificates awarded after the completion of individual courses.

Other Sources of Military-Based Education

✳ Defense Language Institute
✳ Defense Equal Opportunity Management Institute
✳ Defense Acquisition University
✳ Defense Information School

Recording Military-Derived Credit

Credit awarded for military training and/or military experience should be clearly marked as "Military Credit" with the accompanying information from the *ACE Military Guide Online*:

---

[2] *See* <acenet.edu/militaryguide>.

FIGURE 4.4a: Military Course Completions on the Joint Services Transcript

Military Course ID	ACE Identifier Course Title Location-Description-Credit Areas	Dates Taken	ACE Credit Recommendation	Level
	Military Course Completions			

750-BT **AR-2201-0399**   13-MAR-1987 to 07-MAY-1987
Basic Combat Training:
Upon completion of the course, the recruit will be able to demonstrate general knowledge of military organization and culture, mastery of individual and group combat skills including marksmanship and first aid, achievement of minimal physical conditioning standards, and application of basic safety and living skills in an outdoor environment.

• First Aid	1 SH	L
• Marksmanship	1 SH	L
• Outdoor Skills Practicum	1 SH	L
• Personal Physical Conditioning	1 SH	L

(10/00)(10/00)

500-75D10 **AR-1406-0011**   08-MAY-1987 to 26-JUN-1987
Personnel Records Specialist:
US Army Training Center
Ft Jackson SC

To train individuals to maintain personnel records.

• Clerical Bookkeeping	3 SH	L
• Office Procedures	2 SH	L
• Typing	2 SH	L

(8/88)(8/88)

605-19-PLDC **AR-2201-0253**   22-MAR-1990 to 19-APR-1990
Primary Leadership Development:

✳ Assigned ACE number
✳ Dates and name of course or experience
✳ Hours awarded

Special precaution should be taken when awarding military-derived credit to ensure that it is not duplicate credit previously accepted from another institution. See Figure 4.5, "Sample Notation of Military Credit on a Transcript," on page 35, for a transcript showing credit for military education.

CORPORATE EDUCATION

Many businesses provide their employees with workplace coursework and training. Frequently, the employer and the employee request that academic credit be awarded for the training provided. Some larger corporate training programs are accredited, but the majority of programs are not. In either case, institutions must develop their own standards for review, determining what, if any, corporate training and education they will accept for academic credit and post on the academic transcript.

The American Council on Education (ACE) provides a service that assists in the review of corporate training and education: The ACE College Credit Recommendation Service (CREDIT) is an online guide available at no charge. Another source of credit recommendations is the National College Credit Recommendation Service (NCCRS).

The term "corporate education" is also used to describe those programs in which an employer contracts with an institution to provide education,

NONTRADITIONAL WORK AND CONTINUING EDUCATION UNIT RECORDS

33

FIGURE 4.4b: Military Occupations on the Joint Services Transcript

Military Experience				
Occupation ID	ACE Identifier Title Description-Credit Areas	Dates Held	ACE Credit Recommendation	Level
75D10	**MOS-75D-004** **Personnel Records Specialist:**	01-MAR-1996		

Prepares and maintains personnel records or supervises records preparation and maintenance. Prepares correspondence forms and records using word processing software; maintains files; prepares and verifies a variety of personnel records; and provides computer data input.

- Credit may be granted on the basis of an individualized assessment of the student   0 SH   L

(3/94)(4/94)

75Z40	**MOS-75Z-004** **Personnel Sergeant:**	01-MAR-1996		

Supervises the operation of a personnel office, including personnel administration, personnel management, personnel records, and information systems. Supervises performance of legal, reenlistment, and administrative matters as well as personnel actions; reviews, consolidates, and drafts reports and surveys; researches specific policies and procedures related to officer and enlisted personnel administration; reviews data prepared for

often allowing the possibility of earning academic credit. In this case, the receiving institution must determine the specific entity awarding credit and transcribe according to its internal policy.

EXTERNAL DEGREE PROGRAMS

External degree programs allow students to bring together credit from a variety of sources to create a single transcript. Such courses and credits are then applied to a degree program. Institutions offering external degree programs may supplement the credits awarded with traditional coursework of their own to allow students to complete degree programs. Others only provide for the collection of external courses to constitute a degree program and serve solely as the awarding institution. Two examples are Thomas Edison State College in New Jersey and Johnson State College in Vermont. In either case it is recommended that the institution or entity awarding the original credit be indicated on the degree-granting transcript.

CONTINUING EDUCATION

Continuing education provides opportunities for extending education at the postsecondary level. Traditionally, the method of providing this education was via off-campus programs, extension centers, or evening/weekend programs. Today, a large portion of continuing education is occurring online and is often closely associated with corporate training. Continuing education programs may or may not be offered for academic credit.

If continuing education is offered for academic credit toward a degree or certificate, it should appear on the institution's standard academic transcript.

Such continuing education should not be confused with Continuing Education Units (CEU) (*see* "Continuing Education Units (CEU) Records" on page 36).

COMPETENCY-BASED EDUCATION (CBE)

In recent years registrars have seen a surge of literature regarding students demonstrating competencies. Institutions are grappling with how to certify

FIGURE 4.5: Sample Notation of Military Credit on a Transcript

Page **1** of **2**

Name: Sample Student
Student ID: 000001

University of Maryland University College
3501 University Boulevard
East Adelphi, MD 20783

UMUC Official Transcript

--- ACADEMIC PROGRAM HISTORY ---

Program: UG Bachelor's Degree
01/01/2005: Active in Program

Transfer Credits

Transfer Credit from Pensacola State College
Applied Toward UG Bachelor's Degree

		Attempted	Earned	Points
Course Trans GPA 0.000	Transfer Totals	3.000	3.000	0.000

Transfer Credit from Military Service School
Applied Toward UG Bachelor's Degree

		Attempted	Earned	Points
Course Trans GPA 0.000	Transfer Totals	34.000	34.000	0.000

Transfer Credit from NER Military Experience
Applied Toward UG Bachelor's Degree

		Attempted	Earned	Points
Course Trans GPA 0.000	Transfer Totals	6.000	6.000	0.000

Transfer Credit from NEC Military Experience
Applied Toward UG Bachelor's Degree

		Attempted	Earned	Points
Course Trans GPA 0.000	Transfer Totals	12.000	12.000	0.000

that students can apply the skills and knowledge they learn to work situations. Programs are beginning to leverage technology to allow students to learn on their own through online courses, competency-based modules, or open educational resources, guided by faculty facilitators or coaches (Klein-Collins 2014). This in turn may lead institutions to develop programs that no longer use the credit hour as a measurement of education earned. CBE programs offer a range of different kinds of assessments that align with the competencies themselves and require students to apply their knowledge. Because most institutions are still on credit hour systems, some institutions have started building a secondary transcript to reflect competencies in addition to the credit hours earned.

Because competencies do not currently map to the credit hour for financial aid purposes, a standard to define the relationship has yet to be developed. New learning management systems (LMS) are currently being developed to track student enrollment and progress in competency-based programs. Regis-

NONTRADITIONAL WORK AND CONTINUING EDUCATION UNIT RECORDS

35

trars should expect to receive dual transcripts from competency-based programs and begin to develop institutional policies regarding transfer credit, if applicable, for these competencies.

CONTINUING EDUCATION UNIT (CEU) RECORDS

Traditionally, continuing education has referred to lifelong learning opportunities in areas unrelated to a student's formal education. Today, many students use continuing education opportunities to supplement traditional degree programs and enhance their skill sets. Many institutions offer continuing education programs to help graduates embrace lifelong learning, to be better able to accomplish their work and careers, and to become more informed about the world. These programs may allow for professional development, community engagement and outreach, and personal enrichment. It is recommended that a separate transcript be created for continuing education experiences.

CEU vs. Traditional Credit

The traditional standard used by most institutions for academic credit includes a minimum of 750 minutes per credit hour of instruction and generally occurs throughout a 15 week term. Continuing Education Units (CEUs) differ from credit hours and are defined as "contact hours of participation in an organized continuing education experience under responsible sponsorship, capable direction, and qualified instruction (IACET 2015).

A CEU record equates to 10 contact hours of continuing education. If appropriate, a portion of a CEU may be awarded as a decimal value, such as 0.1 or 0.4 CEUs.

CEU Transfer Policies

Each institution sets its own policy in the determination of acceptance of CEUs. Institutions manage the process of a student's request for proof of CEUs similar to the transcript request process, typically through the Office of Continuing Education. Although a paper transcript copy has been the standard method of sending CEU records, electronic format is increasingly the mode of preference.

The CEU Transcript

CEU records are not considered analogous to academic coursework and should not be included on the academic transcript. Elements of continuing education may appear on a co-curricular transcript (*see* "Experiential and Co-Curricular Learning" on page 26).

An individual record for each participant must be maintained by the sponsoring organization or by the institution's designated CEU recordkeeping office. These records are often maintained in the academic records office, but other offices may perform this function as well. A CEU transcript will resemble academic transcripts and include the name of the school, its location, and accreditation with an annotation similar to "Non-Credit Continuing Education Transcript" (*see* Table 4.1, "CEU Transcription Elements and Sample Entry," on page 37). In addition, the following data elements should be included:

* Student name and address
* Student identification number
* Course number and title
* Date of CEU
* Number of CEUs awarded
* Contact hours
* Course subtotals
* Date issued
* A brief description of the program (if applicable)
* Signature of authorized school official

The CEU Certificate

Many institutions issue a Continuing Education Certificate to students upon completion of a specific program. The certificate is a summary of the

Table 4.1. CEU Transcription Elements and Sample Entry

Entry Type	Data to Provide
Course Entry on CEU Transcript	Name and location of sponsoring organization, course number, title of program, date and length of program, qualitative or quantitative evaluation of individual's performance, number of CEUs awarded, and brief description of program itself

Example:

```
AACRAO University Washington, DC Feb. 15-16, 2009
TRAN 111 Transfer Evaluation 1.5 (CEUs)
Satisfactory Participation
A one-day seminar on transcripting college courses
```

name of the program and the number of CEUs awarded using the one CEU per ten contact hours formula. Such certificates are suitable for display in offices, homes, or other locations as appropriate.

Traditional items appearing on a CEU certificate include:

* Name of institution
* Name of student
* "Completed program in..."
* Number of CEUs awarded for the program
* Date of certificate
* Signature of authorized university official
* Seal of institution
* Other (*e.g.*, requirements set forth by the approving body)

5

Transcript Services and Legal Considerations

Tara Sprehe
Associate Dean, Enrollment and Student Services,
Clackamas Community College

Daniel R. Weber
University Registrar,
Northeastern Illinois University

Transcript Services and Legal Considerations

Issuing Transcripts

GENERAL CONSIDERATIONS

Issuing transcripts is a primary responsibility of the Office of the Registrar and/or enrollment services office. A transcript is the official record of a student's enrollment activity and academic efforts at an institution. Providing both official and unofficial transcripts is an essential service to students. Well-organized and easily understood transcripts project an image that inspires confidence in the Office of the Registrar and in the institution as a whole.

TURNAROUND TIME

Prompt transcript service is a hallmark of efficient operation of the Office of the Registrar. While it is recognized that the speed of this service may be impacted during busy periods (*e.g.* the end of a term), the goal should be to produce official transcripts *within one to three working days* from the time the request is received. Normal turnaround time should be referenced when posting information about transcript request and processing procedures. While production time required for both paper and electronic transcripts may be the same, communication to recipients should indicate that receipt of paper transcripts may take longer than those provided electronically.

PROVIDING A WRITTEN STATEMENT OF THE INSTITUTION'S TRANSCRIPT RELEASE POLICIES

A number of institutions and agencies specify the manner in which transcript requests should be processed. Examples include "the official transcript must be enclosed with an application," "a specific number of copies must be included with the application," or "other documents to be mailed to a third party." Specific processing requests of this type may pose problems for some institutions. Hence, it is recommended that colleges and universities have a written statement clearly outlining the transcript release procedures for the institution. Institutional transcript release policies should not be subject to process demands imposed by external entities.

IF THE INSTITUTION CEASES OPERATIONS

In the event of an institution closing its doors and ceasing operations, it is the responsibility of the institution to ensure that its records are moved to a location available to former students. It is important to be familiar with current state regulations, as some states require that an institution designate who will maintain their records should it ever close.

CUSTODIAN OF RECORDS FOR INSTITUTIONS THAT HAVE CLOSED

For those institutions that are charged with the responsibility of maintaining records from an institution that has closed, the following guidelines are suggested:

✳ All records or documents produced should clearly identify the name of the original institution.

✳ All paper documents should be printed on safety paper, preferably with the name of the original institution in the background.

✳ Documents for the closed institution should not bear the seal of the school maintaining the records.

✳ A statement should be included in the key or legend verifying the authority of the custodian institution to provide these documents, such as:

> "At the request of [name and location of closed school], the [name of custodian entity] has accepted custody of the academic records of [name and location of closed school] and has agreed to provide copies of documents contained in those records upon request. The [custodial entity] makes no judgment as to the validity, content, or rigor of any course or program represented on the documents."

More information regarding policies covering the disposition of academic records of closed schools can be found in *AACRAO's Student Records Management: Retention, Disposal and Archive of Student Records.*[3]

TRANSCRIPT REQUESTS

As technology has evolved, students are now able to request transcripts through a variety of methods including internet, email, fax, and in person. Increasingly, institutions have outsourced the transcript request process by contracting with an outside vendor to act as the institution's legal agent. The vendor often collects a fee, processes the student's request, and sends the information to the institution for transcript issuance. It can also provide information that allows the student to track the status of their request. Schools who wish to utilize a third-party vendor to execute transcript requests and fulfillment should understand that even though the vendor is considered an agent of the school, the school is ultimately responsible for the transcript issuance. Schools are also responsible for ensuring that the vendor provides the same level of customer service, security, and confidentiality as the institution.

In accordance with the Family Educational Rights and Privacy Act of 1974 (FERPA), as amended, transcripts usually are issued only at the request of the student. When requests are made in person, appropriate documentation such as a student ID card or driver's license should be required to verify identity. FERPA allows the release of transcripts, without the student's consent, to other educational institutions to which the student intends to enroll.

Interest in genealogy and family history as well as public interest in tragic events, has led to increased requests for transcripts of deceased persons. Because FERPA does not apply to deceased persons, requests from third parties, including the media, should be handled in a manner consistent with institutional policies. For more on FERPA considerations surrounding the release of academic records and information, *see* "Impact of FERPA and Other Federal Statutes on the Release of Student Education Records," on page 48.

Records of student transcript requests, complete with date of issue, recipient, and fee payment, if applicable, should be maintained at minimum for one year. Students should be notified promptly if their transcripts have not been issued because of

---

[3] Available at <www.aacrao.org/bookstore>.

indebtedness (or other holds), inability to authenticate the source of the request, or for other reasons.

RECORDING ATTENDANCE AT MORE THAN ONE SCHOOL WITHIN AN INSTITUTION

For those students who have attended both undergraduate and graduate or professional divisions within the same institution, it is recommended that the entire academic record appear on a single transcript. However, institutions may wish to consider the request of a student to send a transcript with only a specific degree and supporting coursework. In these cases, it is recommended that some heading or other identifying language indicate that this is the academic record for only that particular career or division.

SECURITY FEATURES FOR PAPER TRANSCRIPTS

The sophistication of desktop publishing and other related technologies has made it critical that institutions select paper stock and its associated security features carefully. The paper stock should utilize a color background with an imbedded pattern, preferably the name of the institution. If photocopied, the pattern should drop out and the word "VOID" should appear throughout the paper. A number of other security features are available from paper vendors, including a hidden image that appears only when photocopied or a white signature imposed over the seal that is distorted when copied.

The face of each page of the paper transcript should include the following items:

* Certifying officer/registrar's signature
* School seal
* Date of issue
* FERPA redisclosure statement (in the Transcript Key); see "FERPA Redisclosure Limitation," on page 22.
* Statement that the transcript has been "ISSUED TO STUDENT," when applicable

* Physical description of transcript (see Appendix D, "Sample Transcript and Key," on page 85, for sample wording.)

If institutional policy permits issuing a document other than official transcripts, such as a student or advisor copy, the nature of the document issued should be clearly indicated on each page. Stamps or print lines indicating "Issued to Student for Advising Purposes" are strongly encouraged as "NOT AN OFFICIAL TRANSCRIPT" or "UNOFFICIAL TRANSCRIPT" can be changed to "OFFICIAL TRANSCRIPT" by removal of a few letters. Additionally, transcript alteration is made more difficult if the message covers a portion of the transcript background print (not course entries).

In order to promote the recognition and proper use of official transcripts, guidelines for fighting academic record fraud should be published and included with transcripts issued to entities other than educational institutions. See Chapter 7, "Fraudulent Transcripts," on page 63, for guidelines. If a transcript received is suspected of being fraudulent, the receiving institution is advised to contact the sending institution.

SECURITY FEATURES FOR FAXED TRANSCRIPTS

Although faxing as a medium for the rapid exchange of records and record information is decreasing, properly signed fax requests for transcripts may be accepted as original documents. Generally, transcripts should not be faxed since the document is unprotected in its transmission and arrival at the destination. The quality and readability of a faxed transcript that is on secure stock can often be significantly degraded. Also, it is difficult to verify the identity of the person receiving the fax document.

A faxed transcript may be considered official by the receiving institution subject to its policy secu-

43

rity measures and validation procedures. Absent these safeguards, the receiving institution should consider a fax copy unofficial and use it only until an official transcript, electronic or paper, is received directly from the originating institution.

SECURITY FEATURES FOR ELECTRONIC TRANSCRIPTS

Electronic transcripts provide several added security benefits over paper transcripts. The potential for error in data entry is virtually eliminated, the sending institution can be verified, the date of receipt can be confirmed, and the transcript can be certified as authentic and not having been altered.

Withholding Transcripts

Students may be denied issuance of a transcript due to financial or other institutional obligations (often referred to as holds). The amount of indebtedness leading to non-issuance of a transcript is an institutional decision and policies governing transcript issuance must indicate the impact of indebtedness and other sanctions. Such policies should appear in appropriate institutional publications and websites. Ample opportunity must be provided for the right of review guaranteed by FERPA and by open records laws in some states.

The National Association of College and University Attorneys states that debts to colleges and universities for unpaid tuition accounts and bills (as opposed to student loan debt) may be discharged in bankruptcy, and therefore will be uncollectable after a bankruptcy has been accorded (NACUA 2011). Institutions that continue to withhold transcripts after the debt has been discharged could face monetary or other sanctions. NACUA recommends that "colleges and universities that seek to enforce their collection policies should be mindful how they classify debt, and endeavor to ensure that it is classified as nondischargeable education 'loan' debt" (3).

As in most matters in which litigation could be anticipated, it is advisable to consult college or university counsel before deciding whether to withhold the issuance of a transcript in a bankruptcy situation.

Electronic Transcripts

Students are increasingly able to request that their transcripts be sent electronically, and institutions are able to exchange transcript data electronically with greater ease and frequency by using one or more of the three standard formats that exist: PDF, EDI, and XML. Many institutions have partnered with third-party vendors making the ordering, sending, and payment processes quick and easy for both the student and the institution. At the same time, some institutions are processing transcripts in ways that allow for an institution to load transcript data directly into the institution's student information system versus having to have a staff member enter the data manually.

With these changes, it comes as no surprise that the printing and mailing of paper transcripts is declining. The benefits of electronic transcripts to both the sending institution and the transcript recipients are considerable. An institution's ability to process a received transcript request quicker, a faster response time to the student including the ability for the student to track when the transcript was sent and opened, and increased security measures are a few benefits of electronic transcripts. Electronic transcripts released with the requisite security, safety, and authentication features should be considered and accepted as official transcripts.

WHAT IS ELECTRONIC DATA EXCHANGE?

Electronic Data Exchange (EDX) is a technology using structured data formats and software translators to communicate information between two computer systems. Partners exchanging data agree to use the standard data formats and program their computers to audit documents, transmit them electronically to one another, and notify senders of received documents.

EDX began in the shipping industry more than 50 years ago. Although this technology has come to education more recently, its usefulness has been recognized by a growing number of industries such as banking, insurance, railroad, airline, retail, petroleum, and even research. By the mid-1980s the American National Standards Institute (ANSI) Accredited Standards Committee X12 was formed to develop national standard data formats to be used for a wide variety of applications in traditional EDI. More recently, the PESC-P20W Education Standards Council (PESC) has become the body approving national standard formats in XML, particularly for the education community.[4]

ELECTRONIC EXCHANGE OF PDF STUDENT DOCUMENTS

The fastest growing electronic transcript exchange process uses the Adobe Portable Document Format (PDF). Although the EDI and XML formats have advantages for receiving schools and agencies that need to automate the processing of the transcript data (*see* pages 46 and 47 for information on the EDI and XML formats), a large majority of student transcripts are sent to individuals, companies, agencies, and others who have no need to process the data in the transcript. Students and prospective employers, in particular, are primarily interested in only viewing the document.

In 2013 the AACRAO Standing Committee on Standardization of Postsecondary Education Electronic Data Exchange (SPEEDE) developed its first survey regarding the inbound and outbound processing of PDF transcripts (*see* Appendix F, "Best Practices for PDF Transcript Exchange," on page 91). Survey results indicate that 51 percent of the respondents (n=98) are sending PDF transcripts—with 85 percent of institutions using a third party provider to do so; 85 percent are receiving, and 39 percent are doing both. Those institutions that are receiving PDF transcripts indicate that 91 percent of them accept electronic transcripts from one to five different providers. The number of schools that issue outbound and accept inbound PDF transcripts continues to grow each year as many states, Canadian provinces, and education agencies are mandating that transcripts be sent electronically. Other drivers of this trend include an institutional need to reduce costs (*e.g.* staff, supplies, postage) to operate more efficiently, students' expectation of immediate delivery of their transcript, and a general push to improve student services. Vendors with a long history of service related to academic records and transcripts are partnering with institutions to provide PDF solutions, including electronic transcripts, duplicate/replacement diploma ordering, Apostille processing, etc. Electronic transcript vendors can assist an institution with the creation of a PDF version of the transcript and transcript key/legend by replicating the look of the hardcopy transcript and key. The electronic transcript vendor also assists the institution with embedding the registrar's signature, college/university seal, and other security features into the PDF; providing the ability to determine the active life of the PDF or to deny or restrict the printing of the PDF; hosting the ordering of transcripts; managing the Internet commerce of payments via credit cards; and distributing the transcript in the preferred manner in which the recipient wishes to receive it. Institutions implementing an electronic transcript option for students typically can have the software implemented and be "live" for electronic transcript orders within a matter of weeks after signing a contract.

PDF transcript orders can be accepted and the transcript released within a matter of minutes, thus eliminating the need for rush or express mail ser-

---

[4] The schemas and implementation guide for usage of both EDI and XML are available at <www.pesc.org>.

vices, which is especially useful for transcripts being sent to other countries. Although such things as tracking numbers and registries are useful for insuring the validity and accuracy of a PDF transcript, the practice of digitally signing a PDF transcript is highly encouraged. Although there is an additional fee to digitally sign PDF transcripts, the exceptionally high level of assurance that the transcript is secure and was released from the issuing registrar's office is something that should be strongly considered when weighing the additional cost of a digital signature. Currently, 27 percent of schools use a digital signature, while 49 percent of institutions use a secure website with login, and the remaining 24 percent use encryption.

There is a new PESC standard for PDF that enables one to embed data with the PDF transmission. The receiver would then extract the data (EDI or XML) to use in their student information system and processing.[5]

BEST PRACTICES IN PROCESSING INBOUND AND OUTBOUND PDF TRANSCRIPTS

Best practices for the processing of inbound and outbound PDF transcripts have emerged and, in 2013, the AACRAO SPEEDE Committee issued recommendations related to sending and receiving PDF transcripts (*see* Appendix F, "Best Practices for PDF Transcript Exchange," on page 91). Included as best practices are:

✳ Understanding and selecting the appropriate security for PDF transcripts.

✳ Understanding and selecting the appropriate rights management of the document.

✳ Understanding the various costs associated with transcript orders, and determining the appropriate time to collect the transcript fee.

✳ Accepting secure PDF transcripts as "official" transcripts.

✳ If using an imaging system to capture PDF transcripts, automating the indexing process for improved efficiency.

✳ Becoming familiar with processes for retention and data-mining of transcript data.

ELECTRONIC DATA INTERCHANGE (EDI) STANDARD FORMATS

In 1988, the AACRAO Executive Board appointed a task force to explore the feasibility of creating national standard formats for the exchange of student transcripts directly between educational institutions using electronic media. The task force became the AACRAO SPEEDE Committee. Beginning in 1990, the SPEEDE Committee submitted those proposed standards to the American National Standards Institute (ANSI). ANSI is a private, non-profit organization that promulgates voluntary standards, which become accepted across a wide variety of industries.

ANSI has an "Accredited Standards Committee X12" that focuses specifically on standard formats for the electronic exchange of data.

ANSI ASC X12 has approved Electronic Data Interchange (EDI) standards for various transactions in education including formats to exchange transcripts; to acknowledge that a transcript was received; to process a request for a student transcript; and to generate a negative response to a request for a transcript.

Transcripts sent via EDI allow the transcript data to be sent directly from one computer to a recipient computer with minimal human intervention. This allows the data that make up the transcript to be distributed to various applications in the recipient computer, such as admissions, transfer credit evaluation, etc. Data elements contained in the electronic transcript are clearly defined in the ANSI ASC X12 standards and are explained in the SPEEDE Implementation Guide (1998).

[5] Available at <www.pesc.org/interior.php?page_id=189>.

EXTENSIBLE MARKUP LANGUAGE (XML) STANDARD FORMATS

AACRAO is a founding member of the P20W Education Standards Council (PESC). Established in 1997 as the Postsecondary Electronic Standards Council, PESC is an umbrella group of higher education associations, colleges and universities, software and service providers, and state and federal agencies. PESC develops, approves and maintains standards for electronic data exchange within higher education.

Another format—eXtensible Markup Language, or XML—is an increasingly used data exchange method. SPEEDE has worked with PESC to get the XML standards for the electronic exchange of student transcripts approved by PESC.

Although the EDI format used to send transcripts electronically has a well-established user base and continues to grow, a number of institutions have opted to develop the XML format. XML has gained wide acceptance at postsecondary institutions and is used to routinely transport data of all types. This familiarity with the format and the ease of its use has led a number of institutions to consider an XML format for their electronic transcripts. The AACRAO SPEEDE Committee has developed EDI/XML crosswalks.[6] This would allow users with an existing electronic transcript format, *e.g.* EDI, to translate it to XML and users of XML to translate their transcript to an EDI format. There is an effort to develop a conversion program to facilitate the crosswalk rules for the EDI to XML and XML to EDI but at this time it is far from complete and no free solution exists, although some vendors may be able to convert transcripts and data into the receiving institution's desired format.

BENEFITS AND DRAWBACKS OF PDF, EDI AND XML EXCHANGE

The electronic exchange of PDF, EDI, or XML transcripts provides several benefits over the exchange of paper documents.

✳ *Speed*—In addition to the speed of getting the transcript data from one school to another, the principal benefit is realized by the receiving institution's ability to process the electronic document much faster than a paper document. This is especially true for EDI and XML transcripts as the time involved in opening the mail and entering data from the document into the receiving school's database is eliminated.

✳ *Security and Prevention of Fraud*—Security is greatly improved by exchanging transcript data electronically. Each format has ways to verify that the document came from the institution purporting to have sent it. The sending school is also notified of the date of receipt. The Student Educational Record (Transcript) Acknowledgment is a transaction set available in both EDI and XML to ensure that the original transcript came from the educational institution indicated as the sender and that certain key elements of the transcript were received as they were sent. It also provides the sending institution with confirmation that the original record was received by the intended. Adobe's security features for PDF transcripts, *e.g.* the rendering of a blue ribbon in a blue bar, certifies that the transcript is authentic and has not been altered.

✳ *Communication with Students*—Another advantage of all three formats is that the sending school can advise the student as to when it was sent and when the transcript was received by the recipient.

✳ *Accuracy*—Since information from an EDI or XML transcript does not have to be entered manually into the receiving school's database, the potential for error in data entry is virtually eliminated.

---

6 Available at <www.aacrao.org/home/about/committees/aacrao-speede-committee>.

* *Interpretation of Data*—Data elements contained in the electronic transcript are clearly defined in the EDI and XML standards documents and the EDI and XML implementation guides. This makes it easy to interpret accurately the information received in the electronic data format. Definitions and policies usually included in the key to the paper transcript are specified in the EDI and XML implementation guides.

* *Display of Data*—With the use of a style sheet, a transcript received in XML format may easily be displayed on the receiving school's website for those with permission to view it. The same is true with EDI. Once the transcript data have been received, the receiving school can write a "rendering" program that will display the transcript data in a format of its own design. For transcripts received in PDF format, the electronic transcript typically renders very similarly to the institution's hardcopy transcript so there are no issues with viewing a PDF transcript.

The drawback of the exchange of electronic transcripts lies in the sheer number of methods—and accounts required—to receive and retrieve transcripts from the various vendors (*see* Appendix E, "Sample Electronic Notifications for Transcript Exchange," on page 89).

Impact of FERPA and Other Federal Statutes on the Release of Student Education Records

There are several important federal regulations related to the release of student records. Not only is an institution's compliance with federal law of the upmost importance, it also is the right thing to do. Students expect that when they apply to and attend colleges and universities, the information requested from them will be safeguarded, kept private, and only released either with their written permission,

or as required by law. Here, overviews of the Family Educational Rights and Privacy Act (FERPA), the USA PATRIOT Act, the Solomon Amendment, and the Freedom of Information Act are provided.

IMPORTANT CONSIDERATIONS

It is important to be aware of whether your institution may have committed itself to certain policies that go beyond what either state or federal laws require, *e.g.*, a faster turn-around time for release of student information than the 45 days mandated under FERPA. Additionally, your state may have enacted one or more privacy statutes that might apply to private as well as public institutions in the state. Consultation with your legal counsel is recommended to ensure an interpretation of your institution's policies or your state's statutes.

THE FAMILY EDUCATIONAL RIGHTS AND PRIVACY ACT

The Family Educational Rights Privacy Act of 1974, as amended, is a federal privacy law protecting student education records. FERPA applies to all educational agencies and institutions that receive funding under most programs administered by the Secretary of Education. Since almost all postsecondary institutions, both public and private, receive either grant or federal student aid funding, FERPA applies to almost all U.S. institutions.

Essential Concepts in FERPA
DEFINITION OF A STUDENT

FERPA defines a student as any individual who is or has been in attendance at an educational agency or institution and regarding whom the agency or institution maintains education records. FERPA applies to an entire institution, including cooperative and correspondence study programs, even if only one component (*e.g.*, department or college) of the institution receives funding from the U.S. Department of Education. It is important to remember that when a student either reaches the age of 18 or is attending a postsecondary institution, the rights afforded by FERPA reside with the student, not with the parent or guardian as in K-12.

EDUCATION RECORDS

An education record is defined as any record that contains information that is personally identifiable information to the student and is maintained by an educational institution or by a party acting on behalf of the institution. It does not matter the medium in which the education record is maintained (*e.g.,* paper files, student information system, emails, audio/video files, etc.) or where the record is stored (*e.g.,* on- or off-campus, in the "cloud", etc.). There are several exceptions to what constitutes an education record including sole possession notes, law enforcement records, employment records (unless contingent upon attendance), treatment records, and alumni records.

STUDENTS' RIGHTS

Under FERPA, a student has the right to: 1) inspect and review his/her education records (with some limitations), 2) seek an amendment to education records to ensure that they are not inaccurate, misleading, or in violation of the student's privacy, 3) have some control over the disclosure of information from education records, and 4) file a complaint with the U.S. Department of Education. Detailed information on a student's FERPA rights and how a college or university ensures compliance can be found in the *AACRAO 2012 FERPA Guide.*

DIRECTORY INFORMATION

FERPA allows institutions to release directory information, defined as information that, if released, is generally considered to not be harmful to the student or constitute an invasion of privacy. Directory information typically includes, but is not limited to, a student's name, address, telephone listing, email address, photograph, major field of study, dates of attendance, participation in officially recognized activities or sports, weight and height of members of athletic teams, degrees, honors and awards received, enrollment status (*e.g.,* undergraduate or graduate, full- or part-time), and the most recent educational agency or institution attended.

RELEASE OF NON-DIRECTORY INFORMATION

FERPA contains specific circumstances under which a student's education records may be released without the student's written consent, including:

✳ To other school officials at the institution who have a legitimate educational interest. An institution can include in their definition of school official those contractors, consultants, volunteers, or other parties to whom an institution has outsourced institutional services or functions. If the institution is using an outside party, the party must perform an institutional service or function for which the institution would otherwise use employees, the institution must have direct control related to the use and maintenance of the education records, and the party cannot re-disclose personally identifiable information from education records.

✳ To officials of another institution where the student seeks or intends to enroll, or where the student is already enrolled, so long as the disclosure is for the purposes related to the student's enrollment or transfer.

✳ To determine financial aid eligibility, the amount of or conditions for the aid, or to enforce the terms and conditions of the aid.

✳ To organizations conducting studies for, or on behalf of, institutions, with a written agreement in place.

✳ To accrediting organizations to carry out their accrediting functions.

✳ To parents of dependent students as defined in section 152 of the Internal Revenue Code.

✳ To comply with a judicial order or a lawfully issued subpoena (*see* "USA PATRIOT Act").

✳ In connection with a health or safety emergency. However, the institution must record the "articulable and significant threat" to the health and safety of the student or other individuals, and the parties to whom the information was disclosed.

✳ To the parent of a student under the age of 21 regarding the student's violation of any federal, state, or local law, or of any rule or policy of the institution, related to the use or possession of alcohol or a controlled substance if the institution determines that a student has committed a disciplinary violation.

RECORDKEEPING

An institution must generally maintain a record of each request for access to and each disclosure of an education record made without consent of the student. These records must be kept as long as the record is maintained, need to include the parties who have requested or received personally identifiable information from the education records, and also need to include an explanation of what the legitimate interests the parties had in requesting or obtaining the information. Exceptions to the recordkeeping requirements include information being released to the student, a properly designated school official, a party with written consent from the student, a party requesting directory information, and to comply with a law enforcement subpoena or *ex parte* court order. (*See* "USA PATRIOT Act" below for further details.)

PARENTAL ACCESS TO RECORDS

In certain situations, the parents of postsecondary students may be given access to their student's education records if the student is a "dependent student" as defined by the Internal Revenue Code (*see AACRAO 2012 FERPA Guide*). Because insti-

tutions may, but are not required to, release information to parents in specific circumstances, it is strongly recommended that institutions clearly state in their FERPA policy the circumstances in which parental access may be granted.

USA PATRIOT ACT

The Uniting and Strengthening America by Providing Appropriate Tools Required to Intercept and Obstruct Terrorism (USA PATRIOT) Act amended FERPA on October 25, 2001, to allow for the disclosure of education records to the Attorney General of the United States or to his/her designee without prior consent from the student in response to an *ex parte* order in connection with the investigation or prosecution of terrorism crimes. In responding to a request under this Act, the institution should not record the disclosure made in response to the *ex parte* order. The statute also provides that an institution "shall not be liable to any person" for good-faith disclosure of education records in response to such an order.

SOLOMON AMENDMENT

The "Military Recruiting and Reserve Officer Training Corps Program Access to Institutions of Higher Education" statute, known as the "Solomon Amendment" for U.S. Representative Gerald B.H. Solomon, requires that institutions which receive certain federal agency funding allow ROTC or military recruiters on campus access "at least equal in quality and scope" to other employers. Additionally, the statute allows for student recruiting information to be released to military recruiters for students age 17 or older who are enrolled for at least one hour of academic credit at the institution. If, however, a student has an active "FERPA nondisclosure/block," an institution should not release student recruiting information for that student.

50

Items that Never Can Be Classified as Student Recruiting Information

Items considered as student recruiting information by the Department of Defense include a student's name, address, telephone listing, age (or year of birth), place of birth, class level (*e.g.* freshman, sophomore, etc.), current majors, degrees received, and most recent educational institutional attended. Similar to FERPA, the Solomon Amendment indicates that there are several items that never can be classified as student recruiting information including gender, race, ethnicity, nationality, veteran status, or information on students who have dropped out of the institution.

FREEDOM OF INFORMATION ACT

Many public institutions have experienced an increase in requests from individuals using the Freedom of Information Act (FOIA) to receive directory information on students. Often, these requests are for all of the directory information items for all students enrolled in a semester; however, the requested information may vary. Students who have an active "FERPA non-disclosure/block" should be excluded from the information provided. Institutions are advised to consult with their legal counsel to determine any relevant state requirements when responding to a FOIA request.

Conclusion

It is recommended that institutions weigh all of the above factors when writing policies and procedures around transcript services. In particular, the Office of the Registrar is charged with sometimes conflicting tasks: providing excellent, responsive customer service while maintaining the integrity of academic records. Sound judgment and consultation with colleagues are often the key to success when faced with challenging choices.

51

6

CHAPTER SIX

Security of Student Records

Susan Van Voorhis

*Associate Vice Provost of Academic Support Resources
and University Registrar, University of Minnesota*

Security of Student Records

Years ago, a data custodian only needed to worry about the physical space where transcripts were produced and stored. Today, proper security not only applies to the physical protection of paper records from natural disasters and deterioration, but also to the management of cyber security risks to digital records. These risks can include electronic record alteration, sabotage, accident, negligence, fraud, system conversion, and technological "disasters." The new technologies embraced by institutions to improve the efficiency and effectiveness of the records operation have brought about new security challenges, due in part to the increase in staff required to operate these systems. As the number of individuals who have access to student information systems increases, so do the risks. Monitoring the integrity of the data is critical, as is being able to distinguish the difference between unauthorized changes to data from data entry errors.

Safeguards and Challenges

The regular testing of all aspects of a security system should be ongoing and diligent. In addition, data custodians should determine employees' access to the information in the student information system. The "need to know" test is the best solution: Does the individual requesting access have a legitimate "need to know" the information based on his or her position? Some employees will only need access to view records and others will require "update" access to complete certain processes, which may include the manipulation of course enrollment, grade information, and degree information. The ability to make changes to the academic record should be limited to staff directly responsible for establishing and maintaining the institution's academic records. Strict audit trails on all record entries, and changes of records, must be developed and maintained. The audit trail should be documented either within the system or via a report. Employees and student staff who have access to update student records or their own academic record should have their records audited on a yearly basis.

A procedure for notifying faculty, chairs, and deans of changes in a student's academic status or any grade changes should be established. Institutionally-established emails can be used for this purpose, as well as electronic signature authentication.

Creating standardized reports that colleges or departments can run themselves is also a best practice to allow more control over the decentralization of data. These types of reports include class rosters, grade reports, degree clearance, honors, and probation/dismissal/suspension. By allowing staff and faculty to run these standardized reports, the Office of the Registrar can eliminate the need for each area to create its own report and have access to the student information system. Although this decentralization can be useful, it is important for the people given access to these reports to be trained to understand the Family Educational Rights and Privacy Act (FERPA) (*see* page 48). Checks and balances should be in place to audit the use of this information.

Back-up materials, including tapes, electronic records, and copies of optical images and microforms, should be stored in secure remote locations as a safeguard against loss resulting from natural disasters, vandalism, and human error. Computer-generated transcripts, letters, certifications, and other critical output should be protected by stringent data processing systems security, well-defined office security techniques, and audit trail processes.

System Implementation Security Checks

When implementing new technologies, there are important security steps that involve the data custodian. First, a vulnerability assessment should be performed that evaluates how easy it is to gain unauthorized access to data and how vulnerable the network is to authentication or encryption weaknesses. Additional tests will determine any exposure to server and software attacks. Data custodians should check to ensure systems are compliant with FERPA and other regulations (*e.g.*, PCI and HIPAA).

Encrypted web traffic continues to increase and HTTPS (which is encrypted) makes use of the Secure Socket Layer/Transport Layer Security (SSL/TLS) protocol to secure data across a network. This type of encryption was not built to protect users from malware and botnets. Instead, it addresses the privacy between users and the websites or browsers. In some cases, HTTPS as a transport actually hides the malware and so it cannot be detected.

There are new developments in security architecture that build networks by establishing domains of trusted networks. The links between devices in the domain are secured with the combination of encryption, message integrity checks, and data-path replay protection. It can be very time consuming as a data custodian to keep up with changing technology security practices; however, it is crucial to continue to ask questions to protect against any possible neglect or misunderstanding.

Incident Response Plan

All colleges and universities should have an incident response and communication plan in place. Having a single, designated spokesperson in the event of media questions is the practice at many schools.

Steps to consider in creating an incident response breach plan:

❋ Discover incident or security breach: have one central location to which breaches are reported.

❋ Investigate what was breached and determine if it was non-public data.

❋ Remediate quickly, while being careful not to compromise the machine.
   ◆ Delete hacker tool: take machine offline, but do not wipe any of the contents.
   ◆ Review for other security gaps.
   ◆ Protect against same type of breach.

❋ Evaluate and follow established protocol.
   ◆ Assemble those who perform the forensics (this should be a cross-functional team including data custodians, information technology, media relations, and general counsel representation).
   ◆ Determine steps needed to handle a breach, following state and federal regulations.
   ◆ Coordinate response efforts.
   ◆ Produce a report on the incident.

❋ Contact law enforcement, if applicable.

❋ Notify those impacted with facts about the breach, information about possible impacts and risks, and credit monitoring (defined period of time), if applicable; and the public when appropriate (some states require this by law; and may be required for HIPAA breaches).

* Respond in a timely fashion to inquiries.
* Manage the oversight of limiting a breach.
* Educate the campus community.

Third-Party Vendors

Many colleges and universities are moving to third-party vendors to manage and protect data and produce transcripts. Third-party systems are able to perform many operations and processes on behalf of the institution while keeping costs down. During negotiations with vendors, it is recommended to add the following language to contracts:

* Vendor maintains and reviews a written security program that covers the college or university's data;
* Vendor only uses the data for the sole purpose(s) stated in the contract;
* Vendor promptly notifies the college or university of any potential security incident involving its data and works with the school to address the incident;
* Vendor will comply with both federal and state data security laws; and
* Vendor properly returns or destroys data at contract termination.

Involving the institution's legal counsel is highly recommended during contract negotiations to ensure that the school, its students, and the vendor are protected.

Data Access and Identity Management: Authentication, Use and Protection

As more individuals obtain access to student information systems, reminding them about the "need to know" principle on a regular basis is recommended. Many SIS packages have detailed audits of transactions where individuals can be identified and appropriate use of data can be maintained. It is important to identify which users will need read-only access and those who will need update access. Update access to the system should be limited where possible to protect against misuse or temptation to fraud. Separation of duties and access, where possible, is highly recommended to deter tampering with the data and limit risk to the institution.

Developing a clear and concise plan of how access will be granted will enable a data custodian to monitor those with access to the data. A process document for granting access should include language discouraging the sharing of passwords. Further, developing roles and responsibilities will assist in new employee orientation across the campus and will help if any disciplinary action needs to occur.

Identity management is very important for any college or university to ensure security of its records, as there are many points where failure can occur. Figure 6.1 (on page 58) is a simplified diagram of just a few systems that integrate.

Employees and Desk Space Security

Employees are responsible for their physical workspace, equipment, and access codes as relates to data security. Physical space must take into account the confidential information that may be displayed for others to view. Ensuring that desktops are virus-free protects both the students and the employee. Also, periodic reviews of access rights are necessary as functions and jobs change.

Staff members need to be diligent when using devices that allow them to access data. In addition to keeping equipment up-to-date, it is important not to store protected documents on a local desktop, but instead to keep them in the designated college repository.

Policies and procedures should be updated yearly, and disciplinary action must be taken when a violation occurs. Roles and responsibilities need

57

FIGURE 6.1: Identity Data Flow

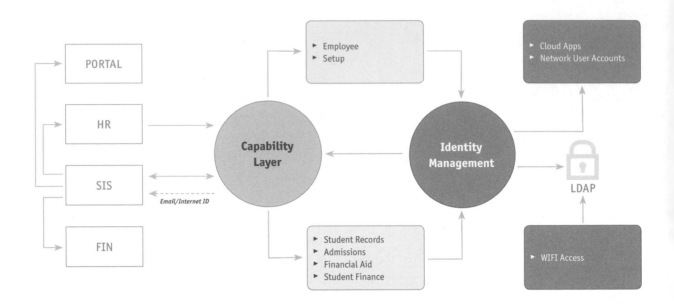

to be defined and presented to staff to eliminate any potential misunderstandings.

Additional ways to keep desktop computers and other devices free from threats include:

* Log out or lock work and personal computers or devices (*e.g.*, iPads, smartphones),
* Restrict remote access to systems,
* Do not open random links (ensure websites are genuine),
* Scrutinize email or attachments from unfamiliar entities,
* Do not download unfamiliar software from the internet unless it is fully vetted,
* Improve data security using encryption whenever possible, and
* Ensure your home network and device are secure.

Questions to consider regarding employee security include:

* Do all of your employees take FERPA training of some kind?

* Do all of your employees sign a confidentiality statement yearly?
* Do you use contractual terms and conditions to ensure that all employees agree to comply with the information security restrictions and obligations that control how they use assets and access information systems?
* Have you reduced the risk of data fraud or misuse of facilities by making sure employees understand their responsibilities and code of conduct? (This should be reviewed yearly.)
* Have you reduced the risk of fraud by making sure that all vendors and contractors understand their responsibilities before they begin working with the data or in the facility?
* Have you reduced the risk of fraud or misuse of data by making sure that staff members in departments other than the Office of the Registrar with access to protected data understand their responsibilities with regard to protecting students?

* Are your organization's security roles and responsibilities defined in accordance with your security policy?
* Do your employees understand that they must comply with the security policy?
* Do your employees understand that assets such as official transcript paper must be protected as well as students' information?
* Do your employees understand the ramifications if security is violated?
* Do your employees lock their desktop when away?

Regular monitoring of transactional activity is important to prevent any security breaches. It is recommended that student employees be audited regularly. This process ensures integrity of the data and eliminates temptations to commit fraud. Documentation should outline disciplinary actions that will be taken if data policies are violated.

Information to enhance staff consciousness of the importance of ensuring the confidentiality and integrity of information include the following:

* *Staff Training Programs*—The importance of maintaining security must be emphasized in staff training programs. This includes not only staff with responsibility for entering and modifying data, but for all other persons having access to such data. Additionally, staff must understand the consequences of any breach or alteration of data.
* *Log-On Screens and Campus-Wide Publications*—Regular reminders of the responsibility for maintaining data security should be included in campus wide publications and log-on screens.
* *Affidavits*—All persons with access to personally identifiable data should be required to sign affidavits acknowledging their responsibility for maintaining record security and recognizing the consequences of security breaches. Department and faculty offices can be particularly vulnerable to unauthorized access to data systems. It is not only records office staff who have access to secured areas, but also cleaning personnel, physical plant employees (such as painters, electricians, etc.), delivery persons, as well as students who come into the area daily. Anyone who has access to secured spaces should also be made aware of the sensitivity of records with which they may come in contact. Standard hiring procedures should include compliance with institutional policies including those involving data security and record confidentiality.
* *Vigilance*—Reminders of the need for vigilance are necessary and appropriate to counteract complacency in regard to record security. Staff carelessness may compromise record security resulting from regular use of personally identifiable data. Special efforts must be made to remind staff members to monitor the physical security of the primary records office and to avoid discussing office matters with unauthorized persons. Discussion of students' records, grades, eligibility, etc., must never occur outside the office.
* *Internal Audits*—To enhance records security, internal audits should be conducted on a regular basis. By periodically checking the integrity of academic records, the registrar and others entrusted with maintaining records security can identify breaches in security in sufficient time to rectify problems.
* *Staff Termination*—A formalized process should be established for employees changing positions within, or leaving, the institution. System and office access needs to be reviewed for those changing positions and adjusted accordingly. A procedure for recovering keys, badges, and restricting access to information and materials should be documented and in place. Passwords, lock combinations, and intrusion alarm codes should be changed each time an employee with access leaves.
* *Violation Sanctions*—Records professionals may wish to encourage the development of state laws

permitting prosecution under criminal codes of persons who make changes to issued transcripts, create bogus transcripts, break the security of data systems, make unauthorized additions/deletions to permanent records, or otherwise alter data in academic records. States are now realizing the seriousness of these crimes, and some state laws are rapidly changing. To determine whether a state has such a law, staff are encouraged to contact the legislative information and research office at their state's capital.

Physical Space Security

Many institutions have gone paperless; however, in some cases paper documents are still necessary. The official transcript, certification and verification letters, and diplomas that are in a paper format need to be secured and protected. Some of these documents contain confidential information and therefore need to be treated with the same protection as any other private data.

Planning and implementation of physical security measures must include not only the principal records office, but all other areas where academic records are maintained and accessed. Planning for physical security must incorporate features that will minimize damage from potential disasters such as fires, floods, tornadoes, pest damage, and earthquakes. Buildings must be inspected to identify the need for sprinkler and fire alarm systems, elevated storage of paper records, reinforced walls, and stabilization of file cabinets, computers, servers, and other equipment. Taking precautions such as these can make the difference between inconvenience and possibly irretrievable loss.

In addition to modifying physical structures to withstand catastrophes, vital institutional records in a paper or microfilm format should be stored off-site in such places as bank vaults, state archive facilities, or businesses that specialize in records storage.

Theft and vandalism can be minimized by limiting distribution of keys to offices, storerooms, and equipment, and by limiting knowledge of vault combinations and computer passwords. Procedures should be established to identify persons entering secured areas and to record times of entry and departure. Alarm systems for secure areas should be connected directly to campus security systems to ensure immediate response to any alarm. The security plan should account for mailboxes, both incoming and outgoing, which are often out in the open and not in a secured space. Wastebaskets can be another area of concern; they should not be used for disposal of records, unless the paper is already shredded. Finally, privacy screens should be considered for computer monitors that may have a public view.

The use of confidential recycling or a secure shredding system to dispose of paper records is recommended. Staff members should not keep personal academic information in an area that is viewable either through a window, in an open area with general public access, or on their desktops.

The following questions will aid an assessment of the quality of physical security arrangements:

* Have campus buildings been assessed for structural integrity?
* Has the spectrum of systems and equipment been evaluated critically to identify potential hazards?
* Are copies of important documents, including microfilmed records and electronic files, stored at remote sites or imaged?
* Have provisions been made for rapid retrieval of backup materials?
* What security provisions are used during working hours? Are they effective?
* Can unauthorized persons view confidential material or hear confidential conversation(s)?
* How secure are offices after regular working hours? If someone enters through a window

or door, will an alarm sound? If so, what will be done?

✱ Do offices have fire and smoke alarm systems? If a signal is emitted, where is the signal heard or sent? Is a routine test procedure in place?

✱ Do staff members know the location of fire extinguishers and fire hoses, and how and when to use them?

✱ Do staff members have specific assignments in the event of fire or other emergency?

✱ Who has keys, card badge access, or the access code to the office? Have all keys been returned by former employees? Are access codes changed immediately after termination? Are entry card badges deactivated? When were the locks last changed?

✱ Are security procedures in effect in the time between office operation and office closure?

✱ Are the offices where records are stored designated as secure spaces with limited access at night by other school personnel?

✱ Has a disaster recovery plan been written? Are copies stored off-site in a secure area to ensure against fraud or loss through accidental or willful destruction?

✱ Are records professionals aware of computer backup schedules and storage arrangements to ensure the accuracy and completeness of the data and the detection of errors?

Supplies and Equipment

Schools that have outsourced the printing of transcripts to a third party vendor must ensure that their paper and the school's integrity are protected. Schools currently printing official documents need to ensure that security paper, stationery, institutional seals, diplomas, signature and certification stamps, and other supplies and equipment used by staff are protected and not accessible to unauthorized personnel at all times. Storing these supplies in a secure place is critical.

To protect this information the following is recommended:

✱ Ensure office area is secure.

✱ Secure and protect all official paper documents from water, fire, pest hazards, etc.

✱ Lock seals, stamps, and other identification items.

✱ Be aware of the environment or unauthorized personnel.

Document Disposal

When they are no longer needed, all documents containing confidential information must be destroyed, in accordance with your campus records retention schedule policy. Confidential information should be disposed of properly by shredding or other methods. AACRAO's *Student Records Management: Retention, Disposal, and Archive of Student Records* can provide information and assistance for crafting a retention and disposition policy for student records.

Summary

Continuing to monitor and work together across higher education institutions—by sharing security best practices and breach scenarios—will help reduce the number of breaches. Incident response and procedure documentation should be reviewed and updated often to ensure an immediate response to any breach of security. Being proactive with security policies and procedures will allow institutions to prevent, interrupt, and/or respond to breach attempts more effectively.

7

CHAPTER SEVEN

Fraudulent Transcripts

Susan Van Voorhis

*Associate Vice Provost of Academic Support Resources
and University Registrar, University of Minnesota*

Fraudulent Transcripts

Transcript fraud is a concern worldwide, and it affects colleges and universities, businesses, employers, governmental licensing boards, and other agencies. Transcript fraud is the fabrication of a document purported to be a transcript from an accredited college or university, an alteration to an officially-issued record, or the inclusion of courses and grades into the transcript which were not earned. Almost any document can be altered, even by a novice, due to desktop publishing and reproduction technologies.

Employers, colleges, and universities must exercise due diligence in verifying credentials of potential employees or students. Technologies, including transcript security paper and the National Student Clearinghouse's enrollment and degree verification services, have helped to reduce fraud and facilitate the credential verification process. Additionally, many schools have defined degree information as directory information unless suppressed by the student, facilitating the confirmation of claimed credentials.

Forging academic information is considered a misdemeanor or felony depending on the state in which it occurs, with penalties varying as well. Institutions that suspect or confirm academic fraud are encouraged to contact their local and/or state law enforcement to pursue investigation or prosecution.

Fraud Perpetrators

Transcript fraud can be done by various sources, including individuals, companies, students, and employees. Institution employees have access to data and tools which can be manipulated for fraudulent use, as do student employees who assist with functions in a records office. Setting up quality assurance processes and transactional reviews will help eliminate attempted fraud, as do yearly audits of staff who have access to update student records. A termination policy for staff members who are found to have altered official records should be in place.

Student fraud has many facets and can take the form of academic dishonesty or altering one's academic history. Academic dishonesty can involve plagiarism of documents or papers and fabrication of information, data, or documents. Students' access to their own academic history through technology can also lead to the temptation to alter their academic record. Fraud also occurs when individuals take the identity and transcript of another student and present it as their own, hurting both the perpetrator and the fraud victim.

As the data custodian of the academic record, it is one's responsibility to ensure its accuracy and authenticity of its history and information, namely that the courses and grades earned in those classes are verified and legitimate. All colleges and universities should have policies and procedures in place to handle the various degrees of academic fraud, including how the outcome may or may not be noted on the academic record.

Some fraud also occurs via companies that are willing to provide students with fraudulent documents for a price. Hiring authorities are becoming more aware of these "diploma mills" and are verifying information through the National Student Clearinghouse, licensing boards, and other record repositories.

As the custodians of the official academic history and records, the Office of the Registrar is essential in communicating about the risks and penalties associated with fraud and in monitoring for such fraud.

Protecting Transcript Integrity

As the data custodian for the transcript, it is imperative that university officials uphold the highest ethical standards to maintain the accuracy and integrity of the student record. Staff members in the Office of the Registrar need to earn the respect of their colleagues at the institution so that when a fraud situation occurs, they have credibility as the data custodian.

As the custodian of the academic record, it is imperative to identify the risks, as well as create, implement, and update a mitigation plan on a yearly basis. Some areas of risk include insufficient staffing, lack of secure storage, office space security, system security, reporting systems, and vendor security.

PROTECTING PAPER TRANSCRIPTS PRODUCED IN-HOUSE

Colleges or universities that produce transcripts in-house must take the following precautions to ensure the potential of fraud is minimized in the paper transcript production process. The process should be documented and reviewed at least yearly. (*See* "Security Features for Paper Transcripts" on page 43 for additional information.)

* Ensure adequate office security (*see* "Employees and Desk Space Security" on page 57).
* Print official transcripts on security paper. The secure paper should meet the following criteria:
  ◆ Institutional identification should appear on the official transcript either before or via printing;
  ◆ Registrar's signature and the institutional seal should be embossed, imprinted, generated, or preprinted;
  ◆ Transcript key should be printed on the back of the paper; and
  ◆ Transcript paper should not be easily replicated.
* Transcript production access, including access to the transcript paper, should be limited. All staff and student employees involved with transcript production should have a criminal background check performed prior to employment and should be provided FERPA training. It is recommended that all staff and student employees sign a confidentiality and appropriate use agreement each year.

SAMPLE PROCESS FOR THE PRODUCTION OF PAPER TRANSCRIPTS

* Mailed, electronic, or drop-off transcript requests are reviewed by an employee. A limited number of staff members should have this responsibility.
  ◆ Review transcript request and information regarding transcript recipient for accuracy and authenticity, following FERPA guidelines (*see* "The Family Educational Right and Privacy Act" on page 48).
* Process the transcript request, ensuring that an audit trail is available.
* Verify student identification and recipient information for quality assurance.
* Record and/or file requestor and recipient information for verification.

* Send official transcript in an official envelope, marked "Official Transcript."
* Include "Issued to Student" on each page of the transcript that has been given or mailed directly to the student.

PROTECTING PAPER TRANSCRIPTS PRODUCED BY A THIRD PARTY

Many colleges and universities contract with third parties to manage requests for and produce official transcripts. Before a contract is signed with the vendor, it is important to have the institution's general counsel review the terms of the contract, as each college or university treats data integrity slightly differently. It is important to establish a process with the vendor that prevents fraud and is documented in either the contract or statement of work (sow).

Suggested contractual items to consider:
* Security of data
  * Security breach ramifications
  * Notification of breach
* Quality assurance review
* Processing time and consequences if timelines are not met
  * Compensation to college or university
  * Compensation to students impacted
* Review of negotiated contract timing
* Pricing vs. production numbers
  * Variable or set
* Right to terminate contract for unsatisfactory performance
* Reporting of performance to college or university

PROTECTING ELECTRONIC TRANSCRIPTS PRODUCED IN-HOUSE

Electronic transcripts provide several added security benefits over paper transcripts. The potential for error in data entry is virtually eliminated, the sending institution can be verified, the date of receipt can be confirmed, and the transcript can be certified as authentic and not having been altered. For electronic transcripts produced in-house, the following precautions should be taken:

* Create authenticity verification process for both incoming and outgoing transfer of transcripts.
* Implement secure transfer of electronic information.
* Create audit trails for quality assurance review.

PROTECTING ELECTRONIC TRANSCRIPTS PRODUCED BY A THIRD PARTY

Third-party vendors should be held to the highest standards, with the following security measures in place:

* Ensure that the vendor is able to protect against fraud by employees.
  * Request vendor's employee ethics and integrity policy and procedure.
* Review vendor quality assurance and security processes for sending electronic transcripts.
* Request fraud protection documentation.
* Request authenticity verification, security protocol, and quality assurance documentation for review.

PROTECTING UNOFFICIAL TRANSCRIPTS PRODUCED BY STUDENTS

Technological advances now afford students access to their academic history and the ability to send unofficial transcripts to potential employers or other schools. With current desktop publishing technologies, students can manipulate, alter, or forge their academic history more easily. Many companies and schools are aware of this potential and have processes in place to prevent or identify such fraud. It is essential that schools or colleges have policies in place for dealing with such fraud and that students be informed of the ramifications of alterating their academic records.

Identifying Fraudulent Transcripts

Transcripts received from other colleges or universities should be reviewed for authenticity. Additional screening should occur if the transcript comes directly from a student or from a non-accredited school. When fraud is suspected, the Office of the Registrar staff should work directly with the presumed sender to investigate the validity of the transcript.

The following "red flag" elements can assist in determining if a transcript has been altered:

* Illogical data elements,
* Unacknowledged attendance gaps,
* Suspect grade changes,
* Blank or missing grades,
* Degree awarded does not appear to match coursework completed,
* Unclear or suspect signature, and/or
* Inaccurate transcript key.

Additional items to verify authenticity if a paper copy is provided:

* Transcript is in official institution envelope with seal present and/or intact,
* Transcript arrived from an accredited institution or vendor,
* Postmark is appropriate to the institution or vendor,
* Security paper is used,
* Transcript key or legend is present,
* Institutional certification is present on the document, and/or
* Transcript has a recent date of issuance.

International Transcript Fraud

Transcripts from international entities are more challenging to check for alteration. Some parts of the world are more susceptible to academic records fraud, such as western and central Africa and the Caribbean. Fake international transcripts are often almost identical to original transcripts, and can include emblems, seals, and high quality paper. The best practice is to require that all incoming official transcripts be sent directly from the issuing college or university or in a sealed "issued to student" transcript. AACRAO provides several resources to assist with international credentialing and verification.[7]

Diploma Mills

There are many entities around the world that produce and sell documents that appear to be academic credentials, such as diplomas, degrees, and transcripts, from what appear to be colleges or universities, but are in reality academically worthless documents from fictitious educational institutions, also known as diploma mills. The following are some possible signs of diploma mill fraud:

* Time to degree: It is unlikely that a degree can be earned in days or weeks.
* Domain that does not end in .edu: While some schools still in the accreditation application process may not have a .edu domain, non-'edu' entities may need to be investigated.
* Complaints with the Better Business Bureau (BBB): Although many accredited schools may have complaints against them it is suggested to review reporting from the BBB.
* Tuition paid on a per-degree basis: Most institutions charge by the credit hour, course, semester/quarter, or the year.
* Website only: Legitimate schools or colleges publish their address/phone and other information on their transcripts or in transcript keys. A school that only provides a website for contact information may indicate fraudulent activity.
* Similar name to an accredited school, such as Hardvard University, University of Britain or Oxford England University.

7 See, for example, International Education Services (ies.aacrao.org) and Counterfeit Diplomas and Transcripts, available at <www.aacrao.org/bookstore>.

✳ Lack of state licensing or nationally or regionally-recognized accreditation: Such information can be verified via the U.S. Department of Education.

✳ Hundreds of degree programs: Many larger reputable schools only offer around 100 degrees.

Using a methodical approach to review incoming transcripts is essential to identifying whether the documents presented are from a real, legitimate, and appropriately-recognized institution.

Survey Results: Official Transcript Practices

In April 2015 AACRAO released the "U.S. Higher Education Transcript Practices and Best Practice Opinions" survey, an update of the 2009 "Transcript Practices, Student ID Numbers, and Name Changes" survey.[1] Recipients of this survey were identified through the 2015 Higher Education Directory (the Directory) using the manpower code of "06" to identify the registrar at each institution. Based on this criteria, the survey was distributed to 2,882 U.S. higher education registrars and one from Palau. Responses represent 839 institutions from all 50 states, the District of Columbia, Puerto Rico, and Palau, for a response rate of 29 percent.

The survey includes two parts. In part A, summarized here, respondents were queried about their institution's official transcript and related database records practices. With few exceptions, most remain virtually unchanged from the 2009 survey. One of the exceptions is the percentage of institutions reporting that they include the entire social security number on official transcripts. The practice declined from 26 percent in 2009 to 13 percent in 2015. In part B, summarized in Appendix B, respondents provided their personal opinions on best practice for official transcripts.

Official Transcript Practices

This section focuses on current official transcript and database practices, including general transcript notations, eligibility to re-enroll, academic probation, transfer credit, honors, and changes in name or gender. Transcript practices specifically related to graduate and professional programs are also reported.

OFFICIAL TRANSCRIPT ITEMS

(*See* Tables A.1–A.6.)

Additional comments about items on the official transcript are reported in *2015 U.S. Higher Education Transcript Practices and Best Practice Opinions* (AACRAO 2015, 24–32). Selected responses include:
* Academic amnesty
* Professional presentations and student teaching experience
* Minor and specializations
* Latin honors
* State education license
* Thesis/dissertation title

---

[1] Full survey results can be found at <www.aacrao.org/docs/default-source/PDF-Files/2015-transcript-practices-at-u-s-institutions %281%29.pdf?sfvrsn=4>.

GRADUATE OR PROFESSIONAL PROGRAM PRACTICES

Sixty-seven percent (n=538) of the 805 respondents indicate that their institution offers graduate or professional programs. Those who responded "yes" were prompted to answer additional questions related to professional program transcript practices. Table A.9 comprises the responses.

Respondents were also asked if their institution is required to list any professional program certifications on the official transcript. Of the 537 who answered this question, roughly one quarter (27 percent, n=145) said "yes". The reasons for the required annotations are contained in Table A.10.

RECORDING NAME AND GENDER CHANGES

(*See* Tables A.11–A.14.)

COMMUNICATION OF ACADEMIC DECISIONS

(*See* Table A.15.)

CREDIT FOR PRIOR LEARNING PRACTICES

Of the 781 respondents who answered the question, 88 percent (n=685) indicate that their institution awards and transcripts credit for prior learning. Respondents were given the opportunity to "check all that apply" for the various methods of annotating credit for prior learning on the official transcript (Table A.16).

TABLE A.1: General Notations

	Yes		No		Total Responses
	n	%	n	%	
Leave of Absence	136	16	691	84	827
Withdrawal from a class after census date	676	81	158	19	834
Courses in progress	700	84	136	16	836
Enrollment status	231	28	594	72	825
Class rank	38	5	791	95	829

TABLE A.2: Eligibility to Re-Enroll

	Yes		No		Total Responses
	n	%	n	%	
Ineligible to re-enroll for academic reasons	315	38	521	62	836
Ineligible to re-enroll for MINOR disciplinary violation	42	5	789	95	831
Ineligible to re-enroll for MAJOR disciplinary violation (*i.e.*, more egregious crimes such as those classified as criminal offenses under the Clery Act)	126	15	702	85	828
Eligible to re-enroll (*e.g.*, in good standing)	212	26	618	74	830

TABLE A.3: Academic Probation

	Yes		No		Total Responses
	n	%	n	%	
Period of time student was on probation	268	32	563	68	831
Indication of probation for academic reasons	391	47	441	53	832
Indication of probation for behavioral reasons	44	5	785	95	829

TABLE A.4: Transfer Credit Information

	Yes		No		Total Responses
	n	%	*n*	%	
Total credits transferred ONLY	373	46	445	55	818
Dates transfer courses were taken	335	41	482	59	817
List each course accepted to transfer	599	73	224	27	823
Indication of applicability of transfer course to major or minor	60	7	756	93	816

TABLE A.5: Honors Information

	Yes		No		Total Responses
	n	%	*n*	%	
Dean's List	514	62	309	38	823
Phi Beta Kappa	80	10	721	90	801
Phi Theta Kappa	129	16	674	84	803
Institution Honor Program	423	52	391	48	814
Departmental or College Honor Program	233	29	581	71	814

TABLE A.6: Degree Completion Information

	Yes		No		Total Responses
	n	%	*n*	%	
Date degree conferred	780	95	42	5	822
Date degree completed if the SAME as degree conferral	332	41	481	59	813
Date degree completed if DIFFERENT from degree conferral	150	18	662	82	812
If you note the date the degree was completed does it include the day of the month?	507	64	281	36	788
Date degree completed, if different from term the degree requirements were met	226	28	575	72	801

TABLE A.7: Student Identification Number on the Official Transcript

	Yes		No		Total Responses
	n	%	*n*	%	
The entire Social Security Number (SSN) or equivalent	105	13	711	87	816
Last 4 digits of SSN	314	39	498	61	812
Another student identification number	652	80	163	20	815
No student identification number	64	8	703	92	767
Full date of birth (month, day, year)	293	37	510	63	803
Truncated date of birth	252	32	540	68	792
Full name	800	98	14	2	814
Other[1]	102	19	436	81	538

[1] "Other" comments include:
- Home address
- Military rank
- Gender
- Maiden name
- Print date

TABLE A.8: Student Identification Number in the Academic Database

	Yes		No		Total Responses
	n	%	n	%	
The entire Social Security Number (SSN) or equivalent	648	82	144	18	792
Last 4 digits of SSN	302	40	454	60	756
Another student identification number	753	95	41	5	794
No student identification number	22	3	719	97	741
Full date of birth (month, day, year)	721	91	72	9	793
Truncated date of birth	104	14	637	86	741
Full name	785	99	11	1	796
Other system-created unique record identifier [1]	177	28	463	72	640

[1] Selected responses include:
- Some departments can only see the last 4 digits or truncates DOB
- Access to SSN in the SIS is restricted by role
- State ID
- SUNY system ID

TABLE A.9: General Notations for Graduate or Professional Program Transcripts

	Yes		No		Total Responses
	n	%	n	%	
Satisfactory completion of institutional qualifying examinations	106	20	424	80	530
Advancement and/or admissions to candidacy	69	13	459	87	528
Title of thesis or dissertation	144	27	390	73	534

TABLE A.10: Reason for Required Professional Program Annotation

	Yes		No		Uncertain		Total Responses
	n	%	n	%	n	%	
Required by state law	44	31	35	24	64	45	143
Required by professional licensing	91	61	16	11	41	28	148

TABLE A.11: Minimally Sufficient Documentation for Name Changes*

	Current Student		Former Student	
	n	%	n	%
Legal proof (*e.g.*, marriage license or court order)	618	74	529	63
One government-issued identification document (driver's license, passport, or social security card)	493	59	413	49
Two government-issued identification documents	148	18	136	16
Marriage license or court order and one government-issued identification	296	35	257	31
No documentation beyond a written request from the student	42	5	80	10
Other [1]	33	4	54	6

* The survey did not require an answer to these questions. As a result, a lack of response could be interpreted as a skipped question OR indicate a negative response. The percentages displayed are the number of positive responses/total possible responses (n=839).
[1] Selected responses include:
- Naturalization document, notarized statement
- Alumni office will accept all types of documentation
- In the case of gender identity, I will accept a written request from the student
- We don't allow name changes for former students
- We only process name changes for former students if it relates to gender reassignment
- The only document acceptable for a legal name change is the social security card issued with the new name
- International student identification card
- For foreign students, only passports

TABLE A.12: Tracking Name Changes in the Database

	Responses	
	n	%
Keep the new name only	41	5
Maintain the former name as well as the new	716	91
Depends on the circumstances [1]	30	4

[1] Selected responses include:
- Birth name is noted
- If the student asks to remove previous names we will
- In most cases we retain both names. If a person is part of a witness protection program, we do not retain the former name.
- We keep maiden names but not "other" names

TABLE A.13: Minimally Sufficient Documentation for Recording Gender Changes*

	Current Student		Former Student	
	n	%	n	%
Court order	449	54	401	48
One government issued identification document (driver's license, passport, or social security card)	207	25	190	23
Two government issued identification documents	69	8	67	8
Court order AND one government issued identification	169	20	153	18
No documentation beyond a written request from the student	79	9	85	10
Other [1]	59	7	68	8

* The survey did not require an answer to these questions. As a result, a lack of response could be interpreted as a skipped question OR indicate a negative response. The percentages displayed are the number of positive responses /total possible responses (n=839).
[1] The survey did not request additional information if respondents replied "Other." This oversight will be addressed in the next iteration of the survey.

TABLE A.14: Tracking Gender Change in the Database

	Responses	
	n	%
Keep the new gender only	428	62
Maintain the former gender as well as the new	196	29
Depends on the circumstances [1]	63	9

[1] Selected responses include:
- We haven't encountered this yet, so our policy has not been established
- We would maintain the former gender name unless we were asked not to by legal authorities or the student
- We are figuring out how best to manage this process
- We will work with students in mid-transition to avoid inadvertently "outing" a student
- We do not currently have a gender change policy

TABLE A.15: Minimally Sufficient Documentation for Communicating Academic Decisions*

	With the Student		Within the Institution	
	n	%	n	%
In-person	251	30	278	33
Signed, hard copy document	521	62	679	81
Communication within a secure portal	382	46	439	52
Institution-issued email	466	56	533	64
Automated workflow	149	18	239	28

* The survey did not require an answer to these questions. As a result, a lack of response could be interpreted as a skipped question OR indicate a negative response. The percentages displayed are the number of positive responses /total possible responses (n=839).

TABLE A.16: Credit for Prior Learning Transcript Annotation Practices*

	Transfer Credit		Institutional (resident) Credit		N/A		Total Responses
	n	%	*n*	%	*n*	%	
Portfolio-based assessment	180	32	162	28	259	45	572
American Council on Education (ACE) guides	407	68	77	13	144	24	600
College Level Examination Program (CLEP) exams	484	75	134	21	68	11	644
DSST Credit by Exam Program	272	50	64	12	226	42	543
Excelsior College Examination Program	144	28	20	4	358	70	512
UExcel Credit by Exam Program	55	11	10	2	425	88	485
National College Credit Recommendation Service	80	16	12	2	407	83	492
Evaluation of Local Training	112	22	74	15	331	65	507
Challenge exam	137	24	237	42	213	38	563
Conversion of institutional MOOC (or other non-credit) to credit	29	6	18	4	436	91	479
Advanced Placement (AP)	549	83	130	20	16	2	660
International Baccalaureate (IB)	438	73	86	14	94	16	601
Other[1]	44	21	21	10	154	72	215

* Although it was intended that "transfer credit" and "institutional (resident) credit" are mutually exclusive categories, some respondents checked both.

[1] Selected responses include:
- German Abitur
- British A-Level exams
- ARTS, SMARTS, JST
- Work experience
- Cambridge program
- FAA ratings to academic credit
- Valley Education for Employment System

Appendix B:

Survey Results:
Opinion on Best Transcript Practices

Below are the responses provided by the participants of the "U.S. Higher Education Transcript Practices and Best Practice Opinions" survey, regarding personal opinion on best practices for official transcripts.[1] Responses represent 839 institutions from all 50 states, the District of Columbia, Puerto Rico, and Palau.

OFFICIAL TRANSCRIPT ITEMS
(*See* Tables B.1–B.3.)

RECORDING NAME AND GENDER CHANGES
(*See* Tables B.4–B.7.)

COMMUNICATION OF ACADEMIC DECISIONS
(*See* Table B.8.)

TABLE B.1: General Notations

	Yes		No		Total Responses
	n	%	*n*	%	
Leave of Absence	222	30	520	70	742
Withdrawal from a class after census date	627	84	122	16	749
Courses in progress	681	90	72	10	753
Enrollment status	336	45	403	55	739
Class rank	79	11	657	89	736

TABLE B.2: Eligibility to Re-Enroll

	Yes		No		Total Responses
	n	%	*n*	%	
Ineligible to re-enroll for academic reasons	448	60	296	40	744
Ineligible to re-enroll for MINOR disciplinary violation	101	14	636	86	737
Ineligible to re-enroll for MAJOR disciplinary violation (*i.e.*, more egregious crimes such as those classified as criminal offenses under the Clery Act	294	40	447	60	741
Eligible to re-enroll (*e.g.*, in good standing)	379	51	358	49	737

---

[1] Full survey results can be found at <www.aacrao.org/docs/default-source/PDF-Files/2015-transcript-practices-al-u-s-Institutions-%281%29.pdf?sfvrsn=4>.

TABLE B.3: Personal Identification Items

	Yes		No		Total Responses
	n	%	n	%	
The entire Social Security Number (SSN) or equivalent	78	11	663	90	741
Last 4 digits of SSN	423	58	313	43	736
Another student identification number	590	81	141	19	731
No student identification number	54	8	618	92	672
Full date of birth (month, day, year)	293	40	435	60	728
Truncated date of birth	351	49	362	51	713
Full name	740	99	7	1	747
Other[1]	39	15	230	86	269

[1] Selected responses include:
- Gender
- Maiden name
- Optional narrative block to explain changes in identity
- Previous names

TABLE B.4: Minimally Sufficient Documentation for Name Changes*

	Current Student		Former Student	
	n	%	n	%
Legal proof (*e.g.*, marriage license or court order)	547	65	498	59
One government-issued identification document (driver's license, passport, or social security card)	403	48	359	43
Two government-issued identification documents	175	21	162	19
Marriage license or court order AND one government-issued identification	273	33	239	29
No documentation beyond a written request from the student	31	4	39	5
Other[1]	13	2	17	2

* The survey did not require an answer to these questions. As a result, a lack of response could be interpreted as a skipped question OR indicate a negative response. The percentages displayed are the number of positive responses/total possible responses (n=839).
[1] Selected responses include:
- In the case of a gender identity issue, I think we should accept a written request
- We do not accept a social security card

TABLE B.5: Best Practice for Recording a Name Change in Database

	Responses	
	n	%
Keep the new name only	13	2
Maintain the former name as well as the new	715	95
Depends on the circumstances	22	3

TABLE B.6: Minimally Sufficient Documentation for Gender Changes*

	Current Student		Former Student	
	n	%	n	%
Court order	453	54	414	50
One government-issued identification document (driver's license, passport, or social security card)	226	27	203	24
Two government-issued identification documents	113	13	99	12
Court order AND one government-issued identification	231	28	208	25
No documentation beyond a written request from the student	85	10	83	10
Other[1]	36	4	37	2

* The survey did not require an answer to these questions. As a result, a lack of response could be interpreted as a skipped question OR indicate a negative response. The percentages displayed are the number of positive responses/total possible responses (n=839).

[1] Responses spanned the spectrum from very permissive (*e.g.*, "There isn't any institutional reason for a school to require any level of justification for changing the gender code") to highly restrictive (*e.g.*, "Do not believe that gender should be changed").

TABLE B.7: Best Practice for Recording Gender Changes in Database

	Responses	
	n	%
Keep the new gender only	228	32
Maintain the former gender as well as the new	456	63
Depends on the circumstances	36	5

TABLE B.8: Minimally Sufficient Documentation for Communicating Academic Decisions*

	With the Student		Within the Institution	
	n	%	n	%
In person	247	30	264	31
Signed, hardcopy document	536	64	654	78
Communication within a secure portal	480	58	564	67
Institution-issued email	442	53	530	63
Automated workflow	275	33	417	50

* The survey did not require an answer to these questions. As a result, a lack of response could be interpreted as a skipped question OR indicate a negative response. The percentages displayed are the number of positive responses/total possible responses (n=839).

Appendix C:

Self-Audit Checklist

The *Academic Record and Transcript Guide* is AACRAO's response to the need for consistency in transcripts produced by postsecondary institutions. This self-audit and the sample transcript and key in Appendix D provide a practical structure within which to implement the recommendations of the Academic Record and Transcript Guide Committee.

We recommend that institutions periodically conduct the following self-audit. All staff members of the Office of the Registrar, and appropriate representatives from other offices, should be included in this process. A more comprehensive self-audit covering all aspects of the Office of the Registrar can be found in AACRAO's *Professional Development Guidelines for Registrars: A Self-Assessment.*[1]

The audit process should also contain a systematic testing of the student database academic history components, especially after a system upgrade or patch, even if that upgrade or patch is not related to academic history. That is, in a test environment, a set of sample former and current student records should be manipulated by changing names, gender, grades, course repeats, posting and unposting degrees, and various other data manipulations that would appear on a printed transcript. A review of

each transcript before and after each process should then be conducted. It is also recommended that the GPA calculation be manually confirmed for a sample set of students.

Are Database Components of Academic History and Transcripts Accurate?

____ GPA recalculation working correctly for term?

____ Cumulative GPA recalculation working correctly?

____ Credits earned for term correct?

____ Cumulative credits earned correct?

____ Attempted term credits correct?

____ Cumulative attempted credits correct?

____ Repeat course function working properly (*e.g.,* in accordance with policy)?

____ Degree posting working correctly?

____ Grade changes working correctly?

____ Academic honors, or other transcripted comments, posting correctly?

____ Transfer or other non-institutional coursework appearing as expected?

---

[1] Available at <www.aacrao.org/bookstore>.

Does Your Transcript Include All of the Components Listed as Essential in Chapter 2 of the Guide?

____ Name, address, telephone number, and website of the institution?

____ Date of issue?

____ Full name of student and student identification number?

____ College credits earned in high school?

____ Accepted transfer credits?

____ Degree sought, major(s), minor(s), certificate(s) program(s)?

____ All courses attempted (*i.e.* both unsatisfactory as well as satisfactory grades) shown?

____ Course type and level clearly identified?

____ Amount, unit of credit, and final grade for each course?

____ Cumulative grade point average (GPA)?

____ Terms/dates of attendance?

____ Narrative evaluation if grades are not recorded in letter or number form?

____ Last entry notation?

____ Statement of graduation containing:

    ____ Degree or certificate received?

    ____ Major, minor, concentrations, tracks, emphases (if applicable)?

    ____ Date degree conferred?

Do You Ensure That the Following are *Not* Included on Your Transcripts?

____ Information listed as "Not Recommended" in Chapter 2, "Database and Transcript Components"?

____ Institutional non-academic information (sanctions for indebtedness, record of transcripts sent, etc.)?

Is Your Transcript Easy to Interpret?

____ Are the abbreviations used for course titles understandable?

____ Are transfer credit summaries or equivalencies clearly labeled?

____ Are graduation data easily located on the transcript?

Are Policies and Procedures for Transcript Services Effective?

____ Is the normal turn-around time as short as possible?

____ Do you periodically check your paper transcript for print and copy quality?

____ Do the official seal, signature, and date of issue appear on each page of the transcript?

____ Do your publications or website identify the conditions under which a student may be denied transcript service?

____ Does a transcript key accompany each official transcript and does it contain the items listed in Chapter 3, "Transcript Key?"

____ Are your academic records and transcript policies in accord with the provisions of FERPA? (*See* Chapter 5)

Are Your Records and Transcripts Secure?

____ Have you recently reviewed the physical security of your office?

____ Do you have security procedures in effect during office hours?

____ Are confidential materials and conversations protected from unauthorized persons?

____ Is the office secure from unauthorized entry when closed?

____ Does the office have burglar, fire alarm and/or fire suppression systems?

____ Do the staff members have specific tasks assigned to them in the event of fire or other emergency situations?

____ Have the locks on the office doors been changed in the past two years?

____ Do you know what persons have keys to the office?

____ Is there a security procedure in effect at closing time?

____ Has a disaster recovery plan been written, and are copies of the plan stored off-site?

____ Are there ongoing programs to keep the staff security-conscious?

____ Do staff and student workers annually sign a statement of confidentiality?

____ If you use safety paper, does it have the recommended security features?

____ If you use safety paper, is it stored in a safe and secure location?

____ Are supplies and equipment used to generate official documents kept in a secure area?

____ Are permanent academic records backed up and stored in another building or off-campus?

____ Are there adequate security measures for electronically-stored data, including frequent password updates as well as routine user audits?

____ Do you regularly challenge your own security system?

____ Do you follow the guidelines in Chapter 6, "Security of Records?"

Sample Transcript and Key

(Please see sample on the next two pages.)

AACRAO Sample University

222 University Drive, Washington, D.C. 22222

www.aacrao.edu (222) 111–3333

Page 1 of 1

```
Student Name   :  Good, Allison
Student ID     :  111111111
Birth Date     :  23 May (day/month)
Print Date     :  2010-01-06 (yyyy-mm-dd)

DEGREES AWARDED
Degree         :  Bachelor of Science
Confer Date    :  2015-12-21
Degree GPA     :  3.767
Major          :  Nutrition

TRANSFER CREDITS
DESCRIPTION                                             HOURS TRANSFERRED
Transfer Credit from SOUTHWEST NEW STATE UNIVERSITY
Applied Toward Science & Engineering UGRD Program
                                Transfer Totals :       16.00
Transfer Credit from NEWER CMTY COLLEGE
Applied Toward Science & Engineering UGRD Program
                                Transfer Totals :       45.00
Transfer Credit from FRESH COUNTY COLLEGE
Applied Toward Science & Engineering UGRD Program
                                Transfer Totals :       13.00
Transfer Credit from WEST OLD A&M UNIVERSITY
Applied Toward Science & Engineering UGRD Program
                                Transfer Totals :        6.00
Transfer Credit from UNIVERSITY OF TORTS
Applied Toward Science & Engineering UGRD Program
                                Transfer Totals :        3.00
Transfer Credit from UNIVERSITY of TORTS
Applied Toward Science & Engineering UGRD Program
                                Transfer Totals :        4.00

BEGINNING OF UNDERGRADUATE RECORD
2008 Spring Term
Major : B.S.-Nutrition

COURSE           DESCRIPTION                ATTEMPTED   EARNED   GRADE   POINTS
BIOL  20233      Basic Microbiology          3.00       3.00      C      6.000
MANA  30153      Organizational Management   3.00       3.00      A     12.000
NTDT  10211      Nutrition & Weight Control  1.00       1.00      A      4.000
NTDT  30123      Nutrition Thru Life Cycle   3.00       3.00      A     12.000
NTDT  40403      Research Methods In Nutrition 3.00     3.00      A     12.000
THEA  10053      Survey of Theatre Arts I    3.00       3.00      A     12.000
                 TERM GPA : 3.625   TERM TOTALS : 16.00  16.00          58.000
                 CUM GPA  : 3.625   CUM TOTALS  : 16.00  96.00          58.000
2008 Summer Term
Major : B.S.-Nutrition

COURSE           DESCRIPTION                ATTEMPTED   EARNED   GRADE   POINTS
SOCI  20213      Introductory Sociology      3.00       3.00      A     12.000
                 TERM GPA : 4.000   TERM TOTALS :  3.00   3.00          12.000
                 CUM GPA  : 3.684   CUM TOTALS  : 19.00  99.00          70.000
2008 Fall Term
Major : B.S.-Nutrition

COURSE           DESCRIPTION                ATTEMPTED   EARNED   GRADE   POINTS
NTDT  20113      Issues Of Food In Society   3.00       3.00      A     12.000
NTDT  20383      Comp Appl Fdserv&Ntr Care   3.00       3.00      A     12.000
NTDT  30144      Quantity Food Production    4.00       4.00      A     16.000
NTDT  30303      Overview/Foodser/Nutr Service 3.00     3.00      A     12.000
                 TERM GPA : 4.000   TERM TOTALS : 13.00  13.00          52.000
                 CUM GPA  : 3.812   CUM TOTALS  : 32.00 112.00         122.000
                 *AACRAO Scholar    *Dean's List
2009 Spring Term
Major : B.S.-Nutrition

COURSE           DESCRIPTION                ATTEMPTED   EARNED   GRADE   POINTS
CHEM  40501      Basic Biochemistry Lab      1.00       1.00      B      3.000
CHEM  40503      Basic Biochemistry          3.00       3.00      C      6.000
NTDT  30313      Food Systems Management     3.00       3.00      A     12.000
NTDT  30333      Medical Nutrition Therapy I 3.00       3.00      A     12.000
NTDT  40363      Community Nutrition         3.00       3.00      A     12.000
RELI  10013      Understnd Rel: World Religions 3.00    3.00      P      6.000
                 TERM GPA : 3.461   TERM TOTALS : 13.00  16.00          45.000
                 CUM GPA  : 3.711   CUM TOTALS  : 45.00 131.00         167.000
2009 Fall Term
Major : B.S.-Nutrition

COURSE           DESCRIPTION                ATTEMPTED   EARNED   GRADE   POINTS
NTDT  40333      Medical Nutr Therapy II     3.00       3.00      A     12.000
NTDT  40343      Advanced Nutrition          3.00       3.00      A     12.000
NTDT  40353      Experimental Foods          3.00       3.00      A     12.000
NTDT  40970      Special Problems            1.00       1.00      A      4.000
NTDT  40970      Special Problems            1.00       1.00      A      4.000
                 Course Topic(s): Data Collection & Analysis
                 TERM GPA : 4.000   TERM TOTALS : 11.00  11.00          44.000
                 CUM GPA  : 3.767   CUM TOTALS  : 56.00 146.00         211.000
                 Undergraduate Career Totals
                 CUM GPA  : 3.767   CUM TOTALS  : 56.00 146.00         211.000

END OF TRANSCRIPT - - - - - - - - - - - - - - - - - - - - - - - - -
```

AACRAO Sample University

222 University Drive, Washington, D.C. 22222
www.aacrao.edu (222) 111–3333
OPE ID 555111-01
registrar@aacrao.edu

Accreditation: AACRAO Sample University (ASU) is accredited by the Commission on Colleges of the Association of Colleges and Schools to award Bachelor's, Master's and Doctoral level degrees. In addition, many of the colleges and academic departments are fully accredited by their individual accrediting agencies. Refer to the University Catalog for further details (www.catalog.aacrao.edu).

Calendar: The academic calendar consists of two long semesters lasting approximately fifteen weeks and one condensed summer semester. Semesters may include several shorter sessions.

Semester Hour: The unit of measure for academic purposes is the semester hour. A semester hour is equivalent to one hour of recitation or a minimum of two hours of laboratory per week for a semester or an equivalent time for a shorter term.

Grading System: ASU uses a four point grading system.

Fall 2010 to Present:

Grade		Quality Points	Used in GPA
A	Excellent	4	yes
B	Good	3	yes
C	Average	2	yes
D	Inferior	1	yes
F	Failure	0	yes
P	Pass	0	no
NC	No Credit	0	no
I	Incomplete	0	no
W	Withdrew	0	no
Q	Admin. Withdrawal	0	no
AU	Audit	0	no
U	Unsatisfactory	0	no

Prior to 2010:

Grade		Quality Points	Used in GPA
A	Excellent	4	yes
B	Good	3	yes
C	Average	2	yes
D	Inferior	1	yes
F	Failure	0	yes
I	Incomplete	0	no
W	Withdrew	0	no
AU	Audit	0	no

Grade Point Average (GPA): A student's GPA is calculated by dividing the sum of earned quality points by the sum of attempted hours for all courses receiving a grade used in calculating the GPA (see above). Only work taken at ASU is used in the GPA.

Repeated Courses: Prior to Fall 2010 and since Fall 2015 only the grade earned in the most recent repeated course is used in the GPA. In the interim period, for the first three total repeated courses only the most recent grade is used in the GPA; if more than three courses have been repeated, all grades in those courses are included in the GPA.

Withdrawal, Transfer, and Bankruptcy: All attempted coursework appears on the transcript. Students may withdraw up until the midpoint of a semester or session. Transfer work must be university level with a grade of at least 'C'. An incomplete becomes an 'F' sixty class days into the subsequent long semester. Students may appeal for academic bankruptcy if they have been separated from the University for at least two years. If granted, all prior coursework will be removed from the GPA and only earned hours will remain on the transcript.

Course Numbering System:

00000–09999	Developmental courses— no credit awarded
10000–29999	Undergraduate lower division courses
30000–49999	Undergraduate upper division courses
50000–59999	Undergraduate and Graduate courses
60000 and above	Graduate Courses

Eligible to Re-Enroll: Academic eligibility to enroll is based upon probation and suspension policies. See Catalog (www.catalog.aacrao.edu).

Transcript Validation and Authenticity: This is an official transcript only if printed on secure purple paper with AACRAO repeated in the background and the official seal appearing as a watermark. Transcripts issued to students will have "ISSUED TO STUDENT" stamped prominently across each page.

When copied the word COPY appears prominently across the face of the entire document. Bleach will turn the paper brown if the transcript is official. Further documentation may be obtained by contacting the university.

Transcript Key Last Revised: 09-24-2015

Appendix E:

Sample Electronic Notifications for Transcript Exchange

Electronic Notification 1

Subject: New File in the/Home/Receive Folder (from <VENDOR>)

New File Notification

A new file from <VENDOR> has arrived into the <RECEIVE TRANSCRIPTS> folder.

Name: TRANSCRIPT_FROM-01234567-A.pdf
Tracking ID: 012345678
Original Size: 8,063 bytes
Uploaded By: <VENDOR>
(secureftp@<VENDOR>.com)

https://ftps.<VENDOR>.com
Regards,
<VENDOR>

Any student information provided is confidential and proprietary to the VENDOR and educational institutions. The privacy of individual students in their records is protected under the Family Education Rights and Privacy Act. Further disclosure is prohibited unless permitted by contract and law.

Electronic Notification 2

Subject: New <VENDOR> Transcript(s) Have Been Delivered

New transcript(s) have been delivered to your secure <INSTITUTION NAME> <VENDOR> mailbox.

Go to <VENDOR>.com and log-in using your email address and password. Note that:

* 24 hours after being opened, transcript(s) will automatically be deleted.
* It is recommended that you download and save the transcript(s) as a PDF document(s).
* Once saved you may verify the authenticity of the PDF document(s).

This email has been sent by <VENDOR> <TAGLINE>

If you have questions regarding this email, please contact <VENDOR, ADDRESS, PHONE>.

Electronic Notification 3

Subject: You Have New Transcripts Ready to Download

Hello <RECIPIENT NAME>,

You have new transcripts and admission documents waiting to be downloaded.

Sign in at exchange.<VENDOR>.com.

You will see the new documents in your Inbox. You can now route the documents to a destination, where you can process and download them.

If you need help downloading the documents, sign in to <VENDOR>, click Support, and you will land at our Help Center.

Would you like to receive more transcripts electronically? We can work with you to bring <VENDOR> to the schools that your applicants are coming from. Please visit the Help Center to contact us.

Thank you,

The <VENDOR> Team

Appendix F:

AACRAO Best Practices for PDF Transcript Exchange

AACRAO and the AACRAO Standardization of Postsecondary Education Electronic Data Exchange (SPEEDE) Committee have been at the forefront of the development of electronic student records exchange. When the AACRAO SPEEDE Committee was first appointed in 1988, computers were still in their infancy and few people owned a home computer. The development of a standard format and server network for the exchange of electronic records was a truly visionary achievement resulting in the first SPEEDE EDI format, released in 1990. It helped pave the way for significant changes in the way student records and data are exchanged, as well as how institutions conduct their business processes. The server network (University of Texas at Austin Server, established in 1997) reached a milestone in January 2013 after exchanging its 35 millionth electronic education record.

In 2008, AACRAO appointed the Electronic Transcript Task Force to examine the current state of technology for electronic transcript exchange, describe best practices, and forecast future developments. One of the conclusions of the report was that while there were well-defined standards and best practices for transcript exchange using EDI (Electronic Data Interchange) and XML (eXtensible Markup Language), AACRAO had not yet developed best practices and guidance for the exchange of transcripts using the increasingly common PDF (portable document format) format. Bob Morley and John "Tom" Stewart also noted in their chapter on electronic records in the *AACRAO 2011 Academic Record and Transcript Guide* that the "production and dissemination of PDF transcripts are not guided by any standards, guidelines, or best practices to date" (71).

The AACRAO SPEEDE Committee was tasked with developing best practices and guidelines for processing PDF transcripts. This document represents that compiled list of best practices for PDF transcript exchange.

Development of Best Practices

A 19-question survey was developed by the AACRAO SPEEDE Committee in spring 2013 to learn how institutions process both inbound and outbound PDF transcripts. The survey was sent to the following distribution lists:

* AACRAO membership via *AACRAO Connect*
* P20W Education Standards Council (PESC) Education Record User Group (ERUG)
* SPEEDE-l listserv

✱ University of Texas at Austin server registrants

The survey closed May 1, 2013 with a total of 98 submitted responses from both Admissions and Registrar areas, with the majority of responses (76 percent) representing the Registrar area.

Survey results were analyzed by the AACRAO SPEEDE Committee and consolidated into the best practices described in this document. For the purposes of this document, the term "Best Practices" represents the results of the survey. Also included are AACRAO SPEEDE Committee member experiences gleaned from approximately 25 years of committee membership (committee mission and goals can be found at the end of this appendix). Committee members represent institutions from across the United States and Canada, and encompass various areas of a college/university, including Registrar, Admissions, Enrollment Management, and Information Technology. Many have been involved with successful electronic data exchange (EDX) implementations at their respective institutions, and have shared those experiences at AACRAO national, regional, and state conferences. Some members are also EDX representatives for their respective state or province.

The AACRAO SPEEDE Committee aspires to foster and expedite the secure and effective transition from paper to electronic sharing of education records in the higher education community. The committee does not endorse any particular third-party provider, company, or organization that offers products and/or services for sending/receiving education records electronically.

PDF Best Practices

The survey showed that 51 percent of survey respondents are sending PDF transcripts; 85 percent are receiving; and 39 percent are doing both. Of those currently sending PDF transcripts, 82 percent use a third-party provider.

Of the respondents receiving PDF transcripts, 91 percent receive PDF transcripts from between one and five different third-party providers.

Of those sending PDF transcripts, 18 percent create their own PDF without the assistance of a vendor service. Institutions creating their own PDF documents should ensure that their security features and process protocols adequately protect the authenticity of the document and student data. In addition, sending institutions should communicate with receiving institutions to build a trusted relationship and ensure acceptance of the PDF document as the official transcript of the student academic record when the previously established process protocols and security standards are followed.

Over the past five to ten years, the number of institutions using third-party providers to process PDF transcripts has increased significantly. This increase may be due to:

✱ Mandates for transcripts to be provided to state and province education agencies and to the United States Department of Education for statewide longitudinal data reporting;
✱ Institutions needing to reduce costs and operate more efficiently;
✱ Students wanting immediate transcript delivery to the destination; and/or
✱ Institutions wanting to improve student services.

In addition to colleges and universities, PDF transcripts are also going to alumni, employers and potential employers, and application centers such as the Nursing Centralized Application Service (NursingCAS) and the American Medical College Application Service (AMCAS). According to the American Council on Education (ACE), PDF is also the format utilized to create the approved Joint Service Transcript, which is the official representation of servicemember military occupation and training. This replaces the former Guard Institute Transcript, the Army/American Council on Education Registry Transcript System (AARTS), and the Sailor/Marine American Council on Education Registry Transcript (SMART). For more information, visit the ACE website (www.acenet.edu/news-room/Pages/Transcripts-for-Military-Personnel.aspx).

Best Practice #1: Understand and select the appropriate security for PDF transcripts.

Survey respondents using a third-party provider indicated the most common method of sending PDF transcripts is via a secure website with login.

According to a PDF white paper published by pdf-tools.com, PDF is appropriate for processing sensitive documents such as student academic transcripts because it supports encryption, access control, and digital signatures. PDF transcripts can be encrypted, which means the contents cannot be reconstructed without knowledge of a password. Various methods for delivering passwords for encrypted files in a separate message ensure security is not compromised.

As PDF technology has advanced to include multiple technologies, the education industry has taken advantage of this more intelligent file format, creating a new PDF standard for the education record. In 2011 PESC developed and approved our next generation PDF transcript. The PDF serves as a container for the embedded XML transcript, enabling data to be sent and extracted as part of the electronic transcript process. This provides the institution the opportunity to ingest the XML data into a SIS or Transfer Articulation System. These PDF documents may also contain other documents in various file formats including, but not limited to, Microsoft Word, media files, another PDF document (*e.g.*, transcript, diploma, course syllabi, dissertation, publications), or EDI.

Survey results showed that only 3 percent of those sending PDF transcripts include embedded XML or EDI. This survey question allowed for additional explanations, some of which are highlighted below:

✳ We are receiving these only from out of our jurisdiction, so the XML is not immediately relevant. However, in general terms I would prefer that the XML was available.

✳ If the embedded XML would allow upload into our SIS system, we would prefer to receive it.

✳ I would prefer to receive embedded XML as it would allow us to take advantage of a "drag and drop" feature of our software to post transfer work.

✳ It would be nice to be able to receive these with key information so they can be electronically loaded either with embedded XML or otherwise.

✳ Depends on how it could interact with Datatel systems...[I]f things such as course descriptions/syllabi are embedded into the transcript, that would be a great time-saver...[and] keep us from having to research the course description...[S]tudent may receive more credit because we can verify all components included in the class.

✳ We run them through an imaging system and then auto articulate through Banner.

✳ I think that I would prefer to [receive embedded XML] because...that might work better with our PeopleSoft system.

FIGURE F.1: Outbound PDF Transcripts

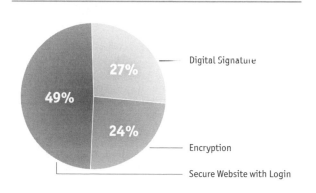

49%
27% — Digital Signature
24%
Encryption
Secure Website with Login

Best Practice #2: Understand and select the appropriate rights management of the document.

Various rights management options are offered by third-party providers of PDF transcripts. Some of the most common options offered are:

* Expire the transcript once opened by the recipient.
* Watermark the transcript when printed by the recipient.
* Limit the number of times the transcript can be accessed or opened by the recipient.
* A combination of the above.

Some key points to consider when selecting rights management options:

* Expiration: If the recipient is an employer, expiring the transcript once opened may be appropriate. However, if the recipient is another institution, expiration of the opened document may cause issues with retaining and/or viewing the academic record in the institution's imaging system or document repository.
* Limit on the number of times it can be opened: If the sender places a limit on the number of times a document can be opened when sending to an institution, this may cause issues if the academic record needs to be forwarded and reviewed by various colleges or departments at the institution.

Of the respondents indicating they send PDF transcripts using a third-party provider:

* 65 percent place an expiration date on the documents.
* 48 percent allow the document to be printed with a watermark.
* 31 percent limit the number of times the document can be printed.
* 17 percent place no restrictions on viewing or printing.

Best Practice #3: Understand the various costs associated with transcript orders, and determine the appropriate time to collect the transcript fee.

If using a third-party provider, most pricing options are similar and may include:

* Base charge per transcript order.
* Additional charge if document contains electronic signature.
* Additional charge for rights management of the document.

The actual charge may occur when the transcript is ordered, when it is delivered, or when it is delivered and opened by the recipient.

Of those institutions that indicated they charge a transcript fee, most apply the charge when the student orders the transcript.

Best Practice #4: Accept secure PDF transcripts as "official" transcripts.

As the rate of acceptance increases, the PDF exchange format becomes more valuable to all institutions. The majority of the respondents that receive PDF transcripts replied "Yes" that they accept a secure PDF transcript as an official document. Some specified various conditions under which they would accept it as official, and some provided reasons that they would *not* accept as official (*see* Table F.1).

FIGURE F.2: Transcript Fee

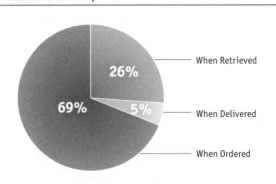

26% — When Retrieved
69%
5% — When Delivered
— When Ordered

TABLE F.1: Survey Responses Regarding Acceptance of Secure PDF Transcripts

Accepted as Official	*Not* Accepted as Official
The PDF transcript was delivered from a verified/secured source	If document is *not* encrypted
The PDF transcript was encrypted/digitally certified	Delivered direct or forwarded from students via email
The issuing institution marked them as "official"	Documents that have been opened or accessed first by another party
Secure email method for those pushed from originating institution or their provider, and the document has NOT already been opened/accessed	Delivered direct or forwarded among colleges within an institution via email

Best Practice #5: If using an imaging system to capture PDF transcripts, use automated indexing for improved efficiency.

Many automation opportunities exist for the processing of PDF transcripts. Some examples are document import, indexing, and even content extraction. Automation can result in reduction of manual errors and potentially decrease processing time. Institutions are advised to identify automation opportunities that make sense based on their process and priorities.

Best Practice #6: Be familiar with processes for retention and data-mining of transcript data.

Third-party providers may offer various options for retention and data-mining. Those using third-party providers to send PDF transcripts should research these options and select those which best meet

FIGURE F.3: Indexing PDFs - Imaging

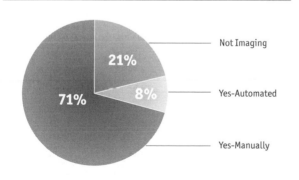

their specific institution's needs and which align with applicable state and federal statutes. Such users should also request to be kept informed of any potential uses of that data.

Common Challenges

The survey respondents were asked, "If you could change your PDF sending (or receiving) process right now, what are the main changes you would like to implement?" The most common responses are shown in Table F.2.

Conclusion

The AACRAO SPEEDE Committee anticipates that these best practices and survey responses will provide some guidance to professionals in the education industry. As we all strive to find more efficient ways to serve our students, we can learn from each other's experiences and those of industry leaders. We appreciate the input and insight from survey respondents and are grateful for the opportunity to speak to Tom Black, Associate Vice Provost for Student Affairs and University Registrar at Stanford University, about his thoughts on the PDF transcript. Tom advocates for the secure exchange of electronic student information through his participation in AACRAO events and was recently featured in the AACRAO *Connect* Spotlight Roundup for the Groningen Declaration. Tom shared these

TABLE F.2: Survey Responses to Desired Changes in Sending and Receiving PDF Transcripts

Sending	Receiving
An increase in the number of institutions that accept PDF transcripts as "official"	A consolidated mailbox from which all inbound transcripts could be retrieved, regardless of the third-party provider
A consolidated common mailbox where all inbound transcripts could be directed, regardless of the third party provider being used; or a standardized process across third party providers	Increased adoption of PDF with embedded XML so data can be imported directly into SIS or Transfer Articulation System
Ability to embed XML	Currently processing XML files but would like to start receiving PDF
Reduced cost structure	Prefer to receive data file (EDI/XML) directly from the UT Server
My institution is not sending PDF transcripts, but would like to	Automation of PDF indexing for imaging

words of wisdom that eloquently sum up the benefits of PDF usage:

> *Standards have their place: to ensure interoperability and service quality. It is a rare occurrence for a standard to spur innovation. The 2011 standard for PDF transcripts is one of those that will encourage changes in the way colleges and universities go about sending the official records. The intuitive nature of the standard makes it acceptable to officials in other nations as well. For a time, the PDF standard will serve us well as we adapt our services for the 21st century.*

Standards require cooperation in order to succeed, therefore institutions must all work together to succeed in providing improved services to our students—simultaneously preserving the integrity of our institutions and student data while leveraging advances in technology.

As PDF transcript technologies and processes continue to mature and additional questions arise, the AACRAO SPEEDE Committee welcomes any questions, comments, and best practice updates at speede@aacrao.org.

AACRAO SPEEDE Committee Mission and Goals

The AACRAO SPEEDE Committee is a professional development committee within the AACRAO national organization. It was formed in the mid-1980s and has since remained active in the coordination, development, and implementation of international exchange standards in the United States and Canada by representing secondary and postsecondary education in collaboration with the standards-setting body P20W Education Standards Council (PESC). The Committee reports to the AACRAO Vice President for Information Technology.

The SPEEDE Committee's mission is to develop, promote, and maintain standards for the electronic exchange of education records, in conjunction with appropriate national standards bodies, through:

* Standards Development and Maintenance
* Promotion and Education
* Training and Implementation Support
* Advisory and Oversight

The Committee aspires to foster and expedite the transition from paper to electronic sharing of education records in the higher education community.

TABLE F.3: 2013 Members of the AACRAO SPEEDE Committee

Robin Greene, Chair	Senior Associate Director, CFNC Pathways University of North Carolina General Administration
Monterey Sims, Vice-chair	Director of Operations/Office of Admissions University of Phoenix
Matthew Bemis	Associate Registrar University of Southern California
Jerald Bracken	Office of Information Technology Brigham Young University
Tuan Anh Do	Assistant Director, Enrollment Management Technology San Francisco State University
Susan Dorsey	Assistant Registrar for Enrollment Services University of Colorado Boulder
Doug Holmes	Programmer Analyst III Ontario Universities' Application Centre
Susan Reyes	Enrollment Services San Diego State University
Shelby Stanfield	Vice Provost and University Registrar University of Texas at Austin
John "Tom" Stewart	Registrar (retired) Miami Dade College

Appendix G:

Survey Results:
Tracking Student Identity Preferences

Introduction and Methodology

The March 2015 AACRAO *60 Second Survey* asked respondents to identify how, if at all, their institution enables students to indicate their identity preferences, including preferred pronouns, preferred gender, and preferred name (Appendix A). The survey was distributed to all AACRAO members, with a total of 880 unique institutional responses.

Respondents represented 16 countries, commonwealths or territories, all 50 states, plus the District of Columbia, and 9 Canadian provinces. All questions in the survey that had yes, no, and don't know/unsure as possible responses prompted those who answered "yes" to check all applicable options for pronouns, gender, and preferred name. The last question of the survey asked respondents to provide additional comments. Several respondents indicated that they are unable to provide the options they would prefer to because the student information system does not support this level of variation. Quite a few also indicated that this topic is under active discussion on their campus and/or about to be implemented as a change in practice.

Results

USE OF PRONOUNS

Only 10 percent (n=90) of responding institutions allow students to select their preferred pronouns. Almost two-thirds do not (n=580) and a further 24 percent were uncertain about the practice. Respondents who indicated "Yes" were asked to check all available pronoun options from a list in the survey and were also provided with the opportunity to list pronoun options not included in the survey (Table G.1). As anticipated, he/him and she/her were the most prevalent of pronoun options (92 percent and 93 percent respectively). Almost 14 percent chose to provide other options not listed in the survey, including "None," "Other" and "Open ended prefix."

ABILITY TO INDICATE GENDER CHOICE

Almost half (49 percent) answered that students are able to indicate their preferred gender identification. Eleven percent were unsure if their institution offered this choice. Table G.2 summarizes the various gender options available at institutions, with 18 percent of respondents indicating other options not listed in

TABLE G.1: Pronoun Options Available for Those Institutions That Let Students Indicate Their Preferred Pronoun

Response	n	%
He/him	86	92
She/her	87	93
They/them	41	44
Xi/xir	7	7
Ze/zir/zim	10	11
Zhe/zhim	6	6
Other	13	14

TABLE G.2: Gender Options Available for Those Institutions That Let Students Indicate Their Preferred Gender

Response	n	%
Male	406	99
Female	404	98
Cis male	4	1
Cis female	3	1
Transgender male	28	7
Transgender female	27	7
Transsexual male	8	2
Transsexual female	8	2
Nonbinary	7	2
Agender	7	2
Other	72	18

TABLE G.3: Indication of Where Preferred Names Can Be Used

Response	n	%
Student identification card	207	45
Class roster	322	70
Transcripts	52	11
Diploma	177	38
Other	138	30

the survey. Similar to the results for the pronoun options, the most common options available are male or female. Very few institutions offer students the ability to select less traditional gender choices.

PREFERRED NAME

Almost two-thirds (61 percent) of respondents indicated that students are able to select a preferred name. Just about 33 percent said "No" and 6 percent were unsure of the practice at their institution. The class roster is the most common location (70 percent) to have the option of a preferred name, with student identification cards (45 percent) and diplomas (38 percent) a close second and third (Table G.3).

Respondents were also asked if the student's legal name is also listed when preferred name is an option (Table G.4).

The mechanisms with which a student is able to indicate his/her preferred name to the institutions varied (Table G.5). Respondents were able to check all that applied and add additional mechanisms. Responses included the student portal, the LGBT office, Student Life office, and a web form, among others.

TABLE G.4: Uses Where the Student's Legal Name is Included with Preferred Name

	Yes		No		Don't Know/Unsure		Total Responses
	n	%	*n*	%	*n*	%	
Student identification card	50	26	119	62	26	14	192
Class roster	115	39	151	51	37	13	297
Transcripts	31	59	17	32	6	11	53
Diploma	26	15	134	79	11	7	170
Other	60	54	47	42	9	8	111

TABLE G.5: Mechanisms for Indicating Preferred Name

Response	n	%
Application for admission	293	62
Through the registrar's office	297	63
Directly to the faculty member	35	7
On the application for graduation	129	27
Through academic advisor	24	5
Other	82	17

Appendix H:

A Framework for Extending the Transcript

As part of the Extended Transcript Track at the 2015 Technology & Transfer Conference, conference participants were presented with the following work done by AACRAO and Student Affairs Administrators (NASPA) to identify emerging practices and develop a framework for an "extended" transcript that represents a broader range of educational experiences than are currently represented by the academic transcript.

In response to increasing funding pressures and a growing emphasis on better equipping a diverse population of students with the skills needed to succeed in the 21st century, institutions of all types are increasingly pursuing new alternatives to the delivery of education. Competency-based education and direct assessment have attracted a great deal of interest among educators and policymakers, but many operational considerations must be addressed when considering these new pedagogical approaches.

AACRAO and NASPA and have been working to bring together registrars, student affairs and other higher education professionals to identify emerging practices in identifying, collecting, and documenting student learning and enabling institutions to officially assert (and communicate) them on behalf of the student. Our goal has been to create a framework

to guide the development of new recording models and operational considerations for higher education registrars and other professionals to share with their campuses, faculty, and academic leadership. These will include examples where institutions have augmented traditional transcripts to present additional information, often in a digital format, as well as those who are creating supplemental documents to include other forms of student learning. Guidance for implementation of these models, including validation of non classroom experiences, student information system considerations, ways to minimize negative impacts to students who transfer, and enhancing the multiple ways students and alumni may wish to present themselves will also be a focus.

The current framework for the academic transcript at colleges and universities resulted from the convergence of academic practice over many years and has largely served as an academic record. The notion of documenting nontraditional learning, learning outcomes and competencies, and co-curricular experiences is at a very nascent stage in higher education. Considerable innovation is taking place at colleges and universities as faculty explore how best to identify and record learning that students are experiencing, create new delivery models and assignments, and develop assessments and rubrics to measure student learning. Rather than attempting to create standards in this rapidly evolving arena, our work should focus on identifying emerging practices, addressing impediments to innovation, and offering creative options for campuses to deliver and document student learning.

Considerations

THE FRAMEWORK SHOULD INCLUDE A CLEAR SET OF DEFINITIONS FOR CAMPUSES TO USE.

＊ There is considerable variation in the terminology used to describe the practices associated with competency and outcome-based education. A basic set of definitions will help avoid confusion when creating transcripts and student records.

CAMPUSES MUST EVALUATE AND DETERMINE WHAT THEY WISH TO INCLUDE AS PART OF AN EXTENDED STUDENT RECORD.

＊ What additional learning activities are recordable? How do we identify the learning that is taking place? How do we measure what the learning is and how significant it is?

＊ Is there a universal way to convey or assign value to the mastery of demonstrable skills or competencies, or the acquisition of knowledge, or what are considered the key elements of the learning experience?

STUDENT RECORDS SHOULD BE MADE AVAILABLE IN A DIGITAL FORMAT.

＊ Digital transcripts and student records provide greater flexibility to capture and display the detail needed to adequately represent outcomes, competencies, and co-curricular experiences.

＊ Students as consumers expect more immediate fulfillment of their requests, which cannot be as easily accomplished with mailed paper transcripts.

＊ To facilitate business process efficiency and student mobility, student transcripts and records exchanged between educational institutions should be made available in one of the current electronic formats such as PDF, EDI, or XML.

＊ Student transcripts meant for employer use should ideally be prepared using interactive technology that offers the user the option to "drill down" deeper into the document as appropriate. New and evolving technology could also support student transcripts sent as data to online portfolios.

＊ If these formats are not available, or do not adequately serve the purposes of the intended constituencies, campuses should be prepared to produce the documents in a PDF format. If the campus intends for the document to be officially issued and verified, it will need to use a secure PDF platform. It is anticipated that the transcript or record could be delivered either in a format that allows the employer to use an affordable technology to obtain needed info (*e.g.* clickable links) or via the established PESC standards for institution-to-institution exchange.

＊ If the university is not planning on issuing a traditional academic transcript it will be important to ensure that the competency or other reports be issued in a secure manner and considered official for purposes of transfer, employment, or acceptance to other gainful activities, like the current academic transcript.

GIVEN THE IMPORTANCE OF STUDENT TRANSFER IN OUR EDUCATIONAL LANDSCAPE, CAMPUSES THAT ARE DEVELOPING COMPETENCY- BASED PROGRAMS SHOULD CONTINUE TO PROVIDE STUDENTS WITH A MORE TRADITIONAL ACADEMIC TRANSCRIPT IN ADDITION TO ANY COMPETENCY-BASED REPORTS OR RECORDS.

＊ Students will likely find difficulty transferring from a competency-based program to a more traditional course-based program, particularly if they transfer before completing the CBE program, if all they can provide is a record of the program competencies. If campuses do not provide a traditional transcript they should be prepared to field questions from the student and receiving institution as they try to place the student appropriately.

* Having information available in sources such as websites and catalogs would help to provide the transfer institution additional resources by which to accurately place the student and determine transfer credit.

* Alternatively, there could be services constructed to capture, search, and interpret information that may be relevant for the translation of expanded records being issued by institutions.

WHILE THERE ARE EXAMPLES OF CAMPUSES USING THEIR DIGITAL ACADEMIC TRANSCRIPT TO CAPTURE AND DISPLAY COMPETENCIES AND LEARNING OUTCOMES, INSTITUTIONS MAY ALSO WANT TO CONSIDER RECORDING THESE IN A SEPARATE, BUT ALIGNED, DOCUMENT.

* Academic transcripts that attempt to capture program-level competencies and outcomes can become complex. This is an area where we look to additional work. Campuses may want to consider separate documents to record learning outcomes and competencies while maintaining the more traditional, but digital, academic transcript. Campuses considering documenting co-curricular experiences may wish to record these on a separate document as well.

* Records could be considered in a modular fashion, allowing the requestor to call for that which will show what and how much was learned, accurately, comprehensively and understandably.

ONE MODEL CURRENTLY BEING DEVELOPED IS FOR CAMPUSES TO CREATE A SEPARATE ACADEMIC TRANSCRIPT, A SEPARATE OUTCOME/

COMPETENCY REPORT, AND A SEPARATE CO-CURRICULAR EXPERIENCE REPORT, BUT THERE COULD BE SIGNIFICANT BENEFITS FOR STUDENTS, EMPLOYERS, AND OTHER AUDIENCES FOR A DOCUMENT THAT PULLS THESE THREE DOCUMENTS TOGETHER.

* The Higher Education Achievement Report (HEAR) in the UK is an example of what is commonly referred to as a diploma supplement. It includes sections on program outcomes and extra-curricular experiences as well as the more conventional academic transcript. There is room for innovation in this area.

The Academic Transcript

The academic transcript in US higher education has evolved over time and guidance has been developed by AACRAO to help provide some consistency in the document. While it may not be necessary for the academic record to serve as the repository of learning outcomes or competencies, there are some improvements that can be made to help ensure smoother student transitions from one institution to another or into the workplace. These enhancements are only reasonably possible if student transcripts are shared electronically.

For example, institutions might consider including course descriptions as part of their academic transcripts by including links to these descriptions from the course titles and number on their electronic transcript or a link to the course catalog from the electronic transcript. Recently the P20W Electronic Standards Council (PESC) has a promising development in the Education Course Inventory. This is a data specification that can capture the level, content, and description of a course, making it much easier to facilitate the transfer of credit. Institutions should designate one central location that serves as a hub for elements such as course descriptions so that linkages will be possible. It will be important to ensure that the location is maintained and updated appropriately, and that older records are archived, so as to ensure the data contained in the link remains accurate. Consideration for records retention policies is also a component with these types of linkages.

An institution could also include linkages to course learning outcomes on the transcript if it chose to do so or have this information available on the university website or other accessible source.

This same concept could be utilized in additional documents such as competency reports by providing linkages within the document that provide access to further information.

Also, there should be a call to fully record other academic activities that are at present being missed by most institutions, or are being awkwardly reported as courses when they are not. Internships, research opportunities, study abroad activities, and community-engaged learning programs, when supervised properly by faculty, deserve attention in the 21st century record.

QUESTIONS:

* Should these digital academic transcripts include links to course descriptions or course learning outcomes?
* Where should campuses keep their course descriptions for the transcript link? On their website? In their digital catalog? In a Word document?
* How can local and cloud-based services be utilized?

Recording Competencies and Learning Outcomes

An emerging practice for campuses developing competency-based programs or who wish to display program-learning outcomes is to create a document or record separate from their academic transcript. Unlike the academic transcript which documents course work completed to date without displaying

what courses remain for the degree (since course selection can vary from student to student earning the same degree), the competency or outcome record could display all of the competencies or outcomes required for the course, program, or even the institution, and indicate whether the student has satisfied each competency or outcome. Schools may choose to use a met/not met mark or some other variation (*e.g.,* high mastery, mastery, not yet mastered) and must ensure that the explanation of the mark is included in the document.

In many respects the competency or outcome record could resemble a degree audit in that it could show the program-level competencies (think of these as requirements or clusters of requirements) and whether or not the student has completed each program-level competency or outcome. These outcomes or competencies may consist of several subcompetencies that will be achieved by various tasks and assessments. In a digital format the record can display what courses, assessments, or rubrics were used to satisfy each competency or outcome. Ideally these would be displayed at the individual student level, particularly if the combination of courses, assessments, and rubrics can vary from student to student. In cases where the individual assessments or demonstrations of learning "roll up" into a competency which then "rolls up" into a program level requirement or competency cluster, utilizing a digital document would allow for expanding and collapsing detail via interactive functionality. Program-level competencies can be provided in a link next to the name of the program that the student is pursuing or has earned.

As an example, schools following the Lumina Degree Qualifications Profile could use the "Categories of Learning" as the program-level outcomes. Under each of these Categories of Learning are numerous proficiencies that make up that category, and these can be documented on this record. A digital format allows for links to richer information such as the courses, assessments, and rubrics that lead to these proficiencies.

Other examples to consider include: Western Governors University, Northern Arizona University, and Southern New Hampshire University.

QUESTIONS:

* Where are the competencies or learning outcomes retained at the institution? What tool will be used to document these? Will students have access to that system? What types of systems are currently being used to store competencies and assessments (*e.g.,* Salesforce, MS Office, Learning Management Systems)?

* Can the competency/outcome record be created out of the degree audit? Can you run both courses and competencies out of the degree audit?

* How do we automate the creation of a competency/outcome record?

* Are there some standards/guidelines that need to be developed in this area, both for transcripting and for records management?

Creating a Co-Curricular Experiences Record

There is growing interest on many campuses in creating a means of representing student involvement and achievement outside of the classroom. Experienced-based learning has become more widespread in recent years, with many institutions accepting experience-based elements as legitimate and valued component of their educational programs (Moore 2013). Unlike a student portfolio where the student selects the content of the portfolio, campuses that are considering creating a co-curricular record must decide what activities or experience should be included in this record. Of primary concern is how these experiences will be validated, who will do the validating, and what qualifies as a legitimate sources of knowledge that should be retained on an academic credential? Will the institution allow a mix of validated and non-validated elements or limit the co-curricular record to only validated areas?

The HEAR report from the UK includes a section on student extra-curricular experiences. This section of the HEAR report has the most variation in format from campus to campus as they develop unique approaches to record these experiences. At the University of Sheffield, their HEAR report includes both recognized campus activities as well as achievement demonstrated through the evaluation of a portfolio. The portfolio review considers achievement in the areas of volunteering, cultural and social awareness, enterprise, job and work experience, and community involvement.

Academically-related co-curricular activities could include such activities as study abroad, undergraduate research, service learning, leadership experience, and internships. In 2010, the National Association for Continuing Education (NACE) conducted a survey that indicated that graduates that took part in an internship program were more likely to receive a job offer than those who did not do an internship. This same population also received higher salaries than non-internship students. However, it is important to note that institutional culture and mission should provide the framework for the co-curricular elements included on a secondary transcript. Other examples of co-curricular practices include student employment, leadership, diversity, and community-based learning.

In addition to identifying the data, quantifying the information is equally important if the goal of the transcript is to provide a more "complete" picture of the student experience. Examples may include using the number of hours to quantify service to an outside organization or hours spent working a summer internship. Another example may be to add student employment on campus and quantify it by paid hours worked in a given term.

UNIVERSITIES THAT ARE CONSIDERING A CO-CURRICULAR TRANSCRIPT SHOULD CONSIDER THE FOLLOWING QUESTIONS:

* What activities should be included in the co-curricular record?
   * Validated experiences that are verified by the institution.
   * Non-validated experiences that are self-reported by the student.
* For those activities that are validated, who will validate these experiences?
* Does the student need to provide consent for everything that appears in this record? If a university chooses to have non-validated elements on the transcript how will those items be submitted and recorded? (Or is there a separate section of the co-curricular record for non-validated, self-reported activities, so the reader of the record can treat them however they deem appropriate?)
* A common concern is that nontraditional students, particularly adult students with family and work obligations, don't have the time to participate in many of the activities that will be recorded in the co-curricular report. How do campuses construct this report to enable nontraditional students to display co-curricular experiences?
   * Are there experiences that are more common for nontraditional students that could be validated through portfolios, prior learning assessments based on their work, military experiences, etc.?
   * Would students be able to record non-university sanctioned activities, such as serving on boards, volunteer activities, etc.?
   * Could a protocol be created at a university to review and validate these experiences?
* Where are these experiences recorded and maintained at the campus? What are the policies surrounding retention of data for this type of transcript?
* If institutions build experience-based components into the curriculum, would transfer students be able to transfer these components to meet degree requirements?

OTHER APPROACHES

* Badges or certificates: Can these be components of degrees or made available to students to document other skills or proficiencies to enhance their degrees?
* Shorter credentials (nano- or micro-credentials and degrees) with defined learning outcomes: Could these be combined and lead to degrees or certificates?
* Visual transcripts: Could these include translations of data into a visual image that students can use in social media?

Glossary

ACADEMIC DISMISSAL OR SUSPENSION: A student's involuntary separation from the institution resulting from failure to maintain academic standards. Academic suspension differs from academic dismissal in that academic suspension implies or states conditions under which readmission will be permitted, while academic dismissal is usually a final decision.

ACADEMIC FORGIVENESS OR BANKRUPTCY: A policy allowing certain portions of a student's prior educational history to be removed from the computation of the student's cumulative credit and grade point average totals. A typical policy includes the removal of all or a portion of the prior academic record from the cumulative totals after a specified period of non-attendance at that or other institutions. Most policies on academic forgiveness or bankruptcy require the student to request this adjustment. Many institutions have a "repeat policy" that allows the first or all prior attempts of the same course to be excluded from the cumulative totals and cumulative grade point average. It is important that the history be removed only from the cumulative totals; no courses or grades should be deleted from the academic record or transcript.

ACADEMIC PROBATION OR WARNING: Denotes that a student's academic performance is below the academic standards defined by the institution.

ACADEMIC RECORD: The unabridged academic history of past and current students at the institution. The record can be in one or more formats including hardcopy, imaged, or residing in a student information system. Typically, this history is maintained by the registrar's office. It contains a chronological listing of the total quantitative and qualitative learning experiences and may include information pertinent to the evaluation of attempted and earned credit.

ACT CODE: A code assigned to colleges and universities in the United States and Canada by ACT, Inc.

CALENDAR SYSTEM: Defines the type of academic session (*e.g.,* semester, quarter, trimester, etc.).

CEEB CODE: A code assigned to colleges and universities in the United States and Canada by the Educational Testing Service and authorized by the College Entrance Examination Board, commonly known as the College Board.

CIP (CLASSIFICATION OF INSTRUCTIONAL PROGRAMS): CIP is a coding structure administered by the U.S. Department of Education, National Center for Education Statistics to classify academic programs by content. It is used in IPEDS reporting among others and is updated every ten years.

CLASS RANK: Class rank describes the position of a student in an academic grouping.

CONTINUING EDUCATION UNIT (CEU): A CEU corresponds to ten contact hours of participation in an organized continuing education experience under responsible sponsorship, capable direction, and qualified instruction. These educational experiences are used to maintain certification in many professional fields. However, CEUs should not be considered analogous to academic course work, and are not included in the academic transcript. *See* "The CEU Transcript" (on page 36) for a listing of data elements that should be recorded on the CEU transcript.

COURSE IDENTIFICATION: Typically includes the discipline or department abbreviation, course number, descriptive title, and number of credits associated with the course. The specific descriptive title should be the same as the one used in that year's catalog. If abbreviations are used, care should be taken to make them intelligible.

CREDIT: The unit used to represent courses quantitatively. The number of credits assigned to a course is usually determined by the number of in-class hours per week, exclusive of laboratory periods, and the number of weeks in the session. One credit is usually assigned to a class that meets 50 minutes a week over a period of a quarter, semester, or term.

CREDIT CONVERSION: Credit conversion from quarter-hour credits to semester-hour credits is accomplished by multiplying the number of quarter-hour credits by 2/3; to convert from semester-hour credits to quarter-hour credits, multiply the number of semester hour credits by 3/2.

CREDIT FOR PRIOR LEARNING (PRIOR LEARNING ASSESSMENT)**:** A policy and system established by an institution to award college credit for learning outside of the classroom. This process involves evaluating and awarding academic credit for learning that is assessed to be similar in content, depth, and breadth to college level learning. Prior Learning Assessment does not represent one single method for evaluation of prior learning. Evaluation may include one or more of the following:

✳ *Experiential Learning Assessments:* also known as individualized student portfolios or interviews.

✳ *Evaluation of Local Training:* program evaluations done by individual colleges of non-collegiate instructional programs.

✳ *American Council on Education (ACE) Guides:* published credit recommendations for formal instructional programs offered by non-collegiate agencies, both civilian employers and the military.

✳ *Challenge Exams:* local tests developed by a college to verify learning achievement.

✳ *Advanced Placement (AP) Exams:* a series of tests developed by the College Board initially for AP high school courses—37 exams in many subject areas.

✳ *College Level Examination Program (CLEP) Exams:* tests of college material offered by the College Board.

✳ *Excelsior College Examination Program (UExcel),* (formerly, Regents College Exams or ACT/PEP Exams), offered by Excelsior College, NY.

✳ *DSST Credit by Exam Program (Formerly known as the DANTES Program):* owned and administered by Prometric, tests knowledge of both lower-level and upper-level college material through more than 30 exams.

DATABASE: In the broadest sense includes all data collected and maintained by the institution in any medium. More commonly, it refers to those items of data, often stored as coded values, that are maintained in the institutional computerized database.

DATES OF ATTENDANCE: The starting and ending dates of a term, a course within the term, or a session. Actual dates (month, day, and year) should be indicated in the database, with term names used on the transcript. If not possible, approximate dates may be designated by the academic year, *i.e.,* Fall or First (or 1) Semester or year. When designating terms as first, second, etc., start with the fall term. For special terms, courses, or sessions that do not fit the traditional calendars, it is even more important that the exact beginning and ending dates (month, day, year) be indicated. Where nontraditional learning is involved, *see* Chapter 4, "Nontraditional Work and Continuing Education Unit Records" (on page 23), for calendar considerations.

DEGREE AUDIT: An analysis (online or printed) comparing the degree and program requirements to the academic history of the student. A typical degree audit program matches the requirements for the student's degree and program with the courses that the student has completed and is currently taking. This frequently includes additional information such as the student's academic status, cumulative GPA, test scores, proficiencies completed, etc. Most degree audit systems also enable advisors and students to run "what-if" analyses to assess change of program decisions and/or confirm completion of degree requirements independent of manual intervention. Future course planning can also be a part of a degree audit system where students plan the courses they intend take in future terms. Academic departments can use these data to optimize the schedule of courses.

DEMONSTRATED COMPETENCIES: Experiences gained outside the classroom for which credit is awarded. Examples include military experience, life experience, CLEP, AP, other nationally standardized examinations, and institutional examinations.

DEMONSTRATED PROFICIENCIES: Typically degree or program requirements such as English or mathematics proficiency, foreign language proficiency, public service, etc., that have been completed by the student. The institution maintains records of these proficiencies in the institutional database, but because credit usually is not awarded, notations of proficiencies are not included on the transcript.

DIGITAL PORTFOLIO: See Extended Transcript.

DISTANCE LEARNING: Courses that take place free of time or space limitations, in whole or in part. Such courses may be offered entirely or partly using a web-based format or a web-enhanced format; or may be delivered through interactive video or other technologies.

ELECTRONIC DATA EXCHANGE (EDX): The electronic exchange of student data currently occurs via three standards: PDF (Portable Document Format), EDI (Electronic Data Interchange), and XML (Extensible Markup Language). PDF is enjoying increased use in transcript exchange. EDI standards are approved by the American National Standards Institute (ANSI) for various transactions, including the exchange of transcripts. XML standards are approved by the Postsecondary Electronic Standards Council (PESC). *See* Chapter 5, "Transcript Services and Legal Considerations" (on page 39), for more information.

ELIGIBLE TO CONTINUE OR RE-ENROLL: A status that indicates the student may continue enrollment or may re-enroll at the institution without any special action required by the student or the institution. *See* "Recording Academic Actions on Transcripts" and "Recording Non-Academic Actions on Transcripts" on page 4.

EXTENDED TRANSCRIPT (ALSO DIGITAL PORTFOLIO): A student-created compilation of co- and extra-curricular accomplishments and interests, stored digitally in any number of formats. *See* "Participation in Co-Curricular or Extra-Curricular Activities," on page 5, and Appendix H, "A Framework for Extending the Transcript," on page 103.

FAMILY EDUCATIONAL RIGHTS AND PRIVACY ACT OF 1974, AS AMENDED (FERPA): An act of Congress that defines the parameters for access to student educational records. Institutional policies and procedures governing release of information about students must be based upon the provisions of the Act. *See* "The Impact of FERPA and Other Federal Statutes on the Release of Student Education Records," on page 48. *See also AACRAO 2013 FERPA Quick Guide* and *AACRAO 2012 FERPA Guide.*

FERPA REDISCLOSURE STATEMENT: A statement recommended to be included on the transcript to comply with FERPA requirements. A sample statement is: "In accordance with The Family Educational Rights and Privacy Act of 1974, you are hereby notified that this information is provided upon the condition that you, your agents or employees, will not permit any other party access to this record without the consent of the student. Alteration of this transcript may be a criminal offense." *See* Chapter 3, "Transcript Key," on page 19 for required items; and "The Family Educational Rights and Privacy Act," on page 48.

FICE CODE (FEDERAL INTERAGENCY COMMISSION ON EDUCATION): Administered and previously maintained by the U.S. Department of Education's National Center for Education Statistics (NCES), it is used to identify institutions of higher education in the United States. However, it has not been maintained by NCES for several decades.

GOOD STANDING: Status often denotes that the student is eligible to continue enrollment or re-enroll.

GRADE: A qualitative rating or evaluation of a student's achievement, most frequently expressed on a letter scale. Grades of A, B, C, and D generally correspond to the terms "excellent," "good," "satisfactory," and "lowest passing quality," respectively. The grade of E or F represents "failure" and

is unacceptable for credit in a course. Some institutions use a plus or minus to further delineate a letter grade. Other grading systems used include 4.0–1.0 scale Pass/Fail, Pass/No Record, Satisfactory/Unsatisfactory, and Credit/No Credit.

GRADE POINTS: Numerical values assigned to letter grades to provide a basis for calculating grade point averages; the most common scheme is the 4-point system: A=4, B=3, C=2, D=1, E or F=0.

GRADE POINT AVERAGE (GPA): An arithmetic ratio denoting the overall quality of a student's academic performance. The GPA is commonly calculated by 1) multiplying the credits for each course by the grade points associated with the grade earned, 2) totaling the points earned for all courses, and 3) dividing the total points by the total number of graded credits attempted, as defined by the institution.

GRADUATION STATEMENT (DEGREE[S] CONFERRED): Identifies on the transcript the degrees awarded by the issuing institution to the student, including dates, majors, and honors, if applicable.

KEY TO THE TRANSCRIPT: Provides information that is needed by the recipient of the transcript to interpret the record properly. It is recommended that the key be printed on the back of the transcript, but it may be a separate document that accompanies each transcript issued.

LAST ENTRY NOTATION: A message or series of symbols signifying that no further entries should follow on a student's transcript.

LOCATION AND IDENTIFICATION OF THE INSTITUTION: Includes the street address, city, state, zip code, and country, if applicable. It may also include other helpful identifying information such as telephone and fax numbers; e-mail addresses; office URL; OPE ID (FICE), CEEB and ACT codes.

MAJOR (PROGRAM OF STUDY): A prescribed number of courses, usually representing between a fourth and a third of the total required for the degree, in an academic discipline. Completion of the major is designed to assure disciplined and cumulative study, carried on over an extended period of time, in a field of intellectual inquiry.

MINOR AREA OF STUDY: A prescribed number of courses, usually about half of the number required for the major, in an academic discipline. Completion of the minor is designed to assure more than an introduction to a specific intellectual field of inquiry.

NAME CHANGES: *See* Name of Student below.

NAME OF THE INSTITUTION: An institution's corporate or legal name. In complex institutions, the names of separate administrative units and their locations may be different from that of the main campus.

NAME OF STUDENT: Includes family name and all given names provided at the time of admission. Nicknames may be included in the institutional database, but should not be used on the transcript. For other name-related considerations, *see* "Name Change Recommendations," on page 7.

NARRATIVE EVALUATION: A written assessment of the quality and characteristics of student performance and achievement. The narrative may stand alone, or supplement conventional evaluation information.

NONTRADITIONAL LEARNING: Varies from traditional classroom work either in its method of delivery (*see* Distance Learning, above) or in its origin outside the classroom (military, experiential, corporate, etc.) For examples of such learning and suggestions for ways to transcript nontraditional educational experiences, *see* Chapter 4, "Nontraditional Work and Continuing Education Unit Records," on page 23.

OFFICIAL TRANSCRIPT: A transcript annotating all academic coursework and any additional pertinent information about a student and issued through a formal process. A paper official transcript should include the college seal or its facsimile, date of issue, and an appropriate signature or facsimile. The paper used should have security features such as a watermark or copy prohibition text to ward against fraud.

PDF: Portable Document Format (PDF) from Adobe allows for electronic exchange of authenticated transcripts. *See* "Electronic Exchange of PDF Student Documents," on page 45.

PRIOR POSTSECONDARY EDUCATION: Includes the names and locations of all colleges and universities previously attended, with periods of attendance, degrees earned, and transfer credits accepted.

QUARTER: A term during which classes are normally in session for ten weeks. An institution on the quarter system usually has three quarters (fall, winter, spring) in the academic year; a fourth quarter may be offered as a summer term.

SECONDARY SCHOOL GRADUATION: Denotes the date of graduation and name and location of the secondary school from which the individual completed secondary coursework.

SECURITY CHECKS: A term that refers to various means of ensuring that data are being stored, encrypted, and shared in a secure and tested manner. *See* "System Implementation Security Checks," on page 56.

SEMESTER: A term in which classes are typically in session for fifteen weeks. In a semester system, there are normally two semesters (fall and spring) in an academic year. There may also be a summer semester or condensed semesters during the summer months.

SPEEDE/EXPRESS: A special task force, appointed in 1988 by the AACRAO Executive Committee, to explore the feasibility of creating a national standardized format to exchange student transcripts directly from one educational institution to another using electronic media. That task force is now the AACRAO Committee on Standardization of Postsecondary Education Electronic Data Exchange (SPEEDE). Committee updates and publications can be found at www.aacrao.org/home/about/committees/aacrao-speede-committee.

113

STUDENT IDENTIFICATION NUMBER: Any unique number (or combination of numbers and letters) assigned to the student by the institution. *See* "Use of Social Security Numbers in the Student Database and on the Academic Transcript" (on page 6) for a discussion of use of Social Security Number as student identification.

TERM: A specific period of the year during which classes are in session. *See* "Quarter" and "Semester" definitions above.

TRANSCRIPT: A document created from the academic record that is used to represent the academic performance of the student.

TRIMESTER: One segment of an academic year, when that year includes three semesters. *See* Semester.

TYPE OF CREDIT: Type of credit should be clearly labeled if credit is awarded on the basis of non-classroom experiences such as military or life experience, qualifying scores on national or local examinations, or corporate education. *See* Chapter 4, "Nontraditional Work and Continuing Education Unit Records," on page 23.

UNOFFICIAL TRANSCRIPT: A document created from the academic record that is issued through an informal process. Unofficial transcripts should not include the college seal or its facsimile, should be provided on paper (or in electronic form) other than that used for the official transcript and should be clearly noted as unofficial.

USA PATRIOT ACT ("UNITING AND STRENGTHENING AMERICA BY PROVIDING APPROPRIATE TOOLS REQUIRED TO INTERCEPT AND OBSTRUCT TERRORISM") (OCTOBER 25, 2001): Allows institutions of higher education to provide—without student consent—education records related to a terrorism investigation, upon presentation of a court order from an Assistant U.S. Attorney General or higher official, certifying that "specific and articulable facts" support the request. *See* "USA PATRIOT Act," on page 50.

XML (EXTENSIBLE MARKUP LANGUAGE): A standard for the electronic transmission of student education records. AACRAO's SPEEDE Committee worked with the Postsecondary Electronic Standards Council (PESC) to set the XML standard for sending and receiving transcripts. *See* "Electronic Data Interchange (EDI) Standard Formats," on page 46.

References and Resources

References

CAEL. *See* Council for Adult and Experiential Learning.

Council for Adult and Experiential Learning. 2011. *Prior Learning Assessment* (Web page). Retrieved from: <www.cael.org/pla.htm>.

Education.com. 2011. *Glossary of Education and Related Articles*. Retrieved January 19, 2011 from: <www.education.com/definition/nontraditional-education/>.

IACET. *See* International Association for Continuing Education and Training.

International Association for Continuing Education and Training. 2011. *Continuing Education Units (CEU)*. Retrieved February 14, 2011 from: <www.iacet.org/content/continuing-education-units.html>.

Klein-Collins, R. 2014. *Assessment's New Role in Degree Completion*. Washington DC: AACRAO.

Mallet, C.E. 1924. *A History of the University of Oxford*. London, Methuen.

Mayhew, B. 2014. Nontraditional education: A view from the market. *Journal of Distance Learning Administration*. (17) 2, Summer.

McDaniel, D. and P. Tanaka. 1995. *The Permissibility of Withholding Transcripts Under Bankruptcy Law, NACUA Publication Series, 2nd Edition*. Washington, D.C.: National Association of College and University Attorneys.

Moore, D. 2013. *Engaged Learning in the Academy*. New York: St. Martin's Press.

NACUA. *See* National Association of College and University Attorneys.

National Association of College and University Attorneys. 2011. Student bankruptcy and the permissibility of traditional campus collection measured. *NACUA Notes*. 9(15).

National Collegiate Athletics Association. 2010. *Nontraditional Courses: How Division I Proposal No. 2009–64 Changes the Initial Eligibility Question*. Retrieved January 19, 2011 from: <www.ncaa.org/wps/wcm/connect/27690180429bd7e693c3f3ca02535edf/2009–64+QA+.pdf?MOD=AJPERES&CACHEID=27690180429bd7e693c3f3ca02535edf>.

NCAA. *See* National Collegiate Athletics Association.

New York State and Civil Service Employees Association Partnership for Education and Training. 2011. *Educational Guide Number 2: Non-Traditional Approaches to Further Education*. Retrieved January 19, 2011 from: <http://nyscseapartnership.org/website/education_guides_1–5/cd_guide2.pdf>.

Quann, C.J. 1979. *Admissions, Academic Records and Registrar Services: A Handbook of Policies and Procedures*. San Francisco: Jossey-Bass Publishers.

SPEEDE. 1998. *A Guide to Implementation of Electronic Transcripts and Student Records, Version 4.0*. Postsecondary Electronic Standards Council: Washington, DC. Available at www.pesc.org.

Resources

AMERICAN ASSOCIATION OF COLLEGIATE REGISTRARS AND ADMISSIONS OFFICERS

The AACRAO website, periodicals, and publications are all sources of practical guidance and information. Here is a selection of resources of most interest to registrars:

AACRAO Website

✱ *Survey Results*—Results of the latest AACRAO surveys of members. *See* www.aacrao.org/resources/research/survey-results.

AACRAO Periodicals

* *College and University (C&U)*—The Association's research journal; focuses on emerging concerns and new techniques; also contains book reviews and practical tips.
* *SEM Quarterly*—Focuses on Strategic Enrollment Management, with additional reports on developments in law, technology, and international admissions.
* *Transcript*—AACRAO's weekly electronic newsletter features a wide variety of articles pertinent to admissions, registration, and current trends in higher education.
* *Connect*—AACRAO's bi-weekly electronic newsletter covers the latest developments in domestic and international higher education and provides information about AACRAO services.

AACRAO Publications

The publications catalog, available at www.aacrao.org/bookstore, lists all publications currently available from AACRAO. These are particularly pertinent to the academic transcript:

FERPA-RELATED

* *The AACRAO 2012 FERPA Guide.* A reference for personnel in higher education containing valuable guidance and training materials to help institutional record-keepers understand and comply with the FERPA, including the latest regulatory changes.
* *The AACRAO 2013 FERPA Quick Guide.* A quick reference on essential FERPA information, designed to give staff and faculty members key facts on their role in FERPA compliance.

FRAUDULENT ACADEMIC CREDENTIALS

* *Counterfeit Diplomas and Transcripts.* Gives educators the tools needed to aggressively protect the legitimacy of their documents; helps employers evaluate credentials of new hires; explores existing state and federal statutes that may provide relief against injury done to institutions by document counterfeiters.
* *Accreditation Mills.* Explores the growing influence and threat of accreditation fraud, and includes a valuable list of state and federal authorities and specific names of false accreditors that can be utilized to protect institutions from becoming victims of fraud.
* *Guide to Bogus Institutions and Documents.* Gives tools and techniques to detect bogus institutions and documents, offers guidelines in handling cases of fraud, and helps professionals prevent their institution or organization from becoming a victim of fraud.

RECORD AND REGISTRATION

* *AACRAO's Student Records Management: Retention, Disposal, and Archive of Student Records.* Includes retention schedule for applicants who do not enroll and a retention schedule for admissions records for applicants who enroll; also includes policies covering disposition of academic records of closed schools.
* *Electronic Data Exchange Primer.* Addresses the most commonly asked questions regarding electronic data exchanges, including matters relating to both traditional EDI standards and contemporary XML data standards as shaped by the Postsecondary Electronic Standards Council (PESC).

SELF-AUDIT

* *AACRAO's Professional Development Guidelines for Registrars: A Self-Assessment.* Featured Sections include: "Electronic Communication;" "Transcript Processes and Procedures;" "Information Technology and Support Equipment;" and "Legal Issues" (FERPA; Solomon Amendment; and Student Right-to-Know Act). *See* AACRAO's website for ongoing updates.

AACRAO Professional Development

AACRAO offers highly focused meetings, workshops and webinars to help keep you current with the latest in enrollment management, records and registration, information technology, and student services. *See* www.aacrao.org/professional-development.

AMERICAN COUNCIL ON EDUCATION (ACE)

✻ *College Credit Recommendation Service (CREDIT).* *See* www.acenet.edu/news-room/Pages/College-Credit-Recommendation-Service-CREDIT.aspx.

✻ *ACE Military Guide Online*—Presents the *Guide to the Evaluation of Educational Experiences in the Armed Services* in an online format. *See* www.acenct.edu/news-room/Pages/Military-Guide-Online.aspx.

"FINDLAW"

✻ An excellent public resource for finding laws, regulations, and caselaw at the state and federal level, and internationally. *See* www.findlaw.com.

Index